EXAMINE

THE END TIMES

EXAMINE THE END TIMES

JOSEPH MALARA

www.josephmalara.com

Contents edited by: Aimee Malara

Cover design by: Joseph Malara

Written by: Joseph Malara

ISBN: 979-8-9859553-3-0

WWW.JOSEPHMALARA.COM

JosephMalara@yahoo.com

MALARA HAS ALSO WRITTEN:

- God's Clarity Through Poetry
- *God's Clarity Through Poetry 2*
- The Bible on How to Box
- *Celebrity Sculptures & Hands of Stone, My Story*
- Digging Deeper into God's Truth Defines a Christian
- *The Guide to Christian Dating, Marriage and Sex*
- IT'S ALL SUBJECT TO GOD'S WORD

And this book

Examine The End Times

ISBN: 979-8-9859553-3-0

www.JosephMalara.com

JosephMalara@yahoo.com

Contents

Acknowledgments

I thank Father God for whatever reason He had to choose me to be Saved. I am so grateful and so unworthy. I am infinitely indebted to my Savior Jesus Christ, who paid my debt, which I couldn't. I thank The Holy Spirit for quickening my heart. He has equipped and gifted me with His comfort, discernment, and writing wisdom. In doing so, I pray I represent God's Truths, not mine. I also thank God for giving me such a beautiful, wise, and Godly wife, she is priceless. Indeed, with God and Aimee, our days are full of His Mercy and His Grace. He has given me an eagerness to learn more and more about HIM. In life when one loves God and His Word, it is a life of dealing with many who hate and distance themselves from us; it is a narrow road. However, a road I would never leave, nor could I. It is NOT my grip on Him, but His grip on me that keeps me. His unfathomable Agape Love is the most difficult to understand.

Above all, the love from Him conveyed through His Word is incomprehensible. It drives me and my wife to love Him more and more with each passing day...

Introduction

What's the most intriguing subject to most people in the world today, Christian and non-Christian? It's to "Examine The End Times", Eschatology, **Going back to the future!** Why are so many fascinated by what is to come? Possibly it's our human nature of curiosity, as we want to know, NO, we MUST know! **We want to discern our own End Time in Heaven or Hell and our Earth's End Time.** Regrettably, most have been greatly deceived by devilish liars, false teachers, and countless fanatical charlatans. **The Book of Revelation is the least-read book in the Bible. It is also the most misunderstood and misinterpreted, book.** This was my driving force behind the writing of this most important and captivating book. It's been asked of me numerous times "How Does it ALL End?" Are we in The End Times now? What will happen next? **Why isn't America in the Bible?** What will become of the Earth; what will be its real demise? What does God's Word say will happen when I die? **These are the most thought-provoking topics known to man.** Those who love God and those who hate and reject the God of The Bible, reject Jesus as The Christ. Everyone is watching, waiting, praying, and hoping for epic Biblical answers. **What's next**, The Antichrist, The Mark of The Beast, The Rapture, The War of Armageddon, Jesus's Return, Judgment Day, or a Supernatural Disaster? What are the differences between the birth pains of the Rapture and the birth pains of the 2nd Coming? **This book also includes my verse-by-verse commentary on the Book of Revelation**, using the King James Bible. I drop a pebble into the pond of this book and the ripples speak volumes... A sure sign of the times and a true Blessing awaits YOU as you read all about the unveiling of the mysteries of God, through The Book of Revelation...

I

Where are the Answers?

Let's suppose YOU love Jesus even a little bit before reading this book. Afterward, you will love Him much more than you ever thought possible. Then again, if YOU don't love Him too much today, by the end of this book YOU will HATE HIM without a cause. Read this book with no personal presuppositions of past religious experiences or traditions. This book submits to and exposes the cold hard Biblical Truths of the End Times. Yet, it will do it in a way that the average "Joe" will understand.

Where in God's Holy Word do we find the answers to our many questions of The End Times, termed Eschatology? We now know that over 300 Bible prophecies were fulfilled in the life and death of Christ alone! There are well over 1000 prophecies in the 66 books of the Bible; yes, even more, have all come to fruition. In the writing of this book, <u>other than the verses specified</u> I used the **KJV** King James Version Bible. Then, for clarity, I will use the Biblical word **"Elect".** This encompasses all those **Born Again by God, through HIS Salvific Love** e.g., *God's Elect, God's Chosen, His Church, His Bride, Tribulation Saints, Old Testament Saints, Anointed, Sheep, Redeemed, In Christ, True Believer, Saved, Body of Christ,* and *Body of Believers.* I will make distinctions as needed. I will use the idiom **"The 2nd Coming"** in this book in place of these titles; *The Day of The Lord,* aka *His Return,* aka *Great and Dreadful Day of The Lord,* aka *The Day of Doom,* and aka *The 2nd Advent.* In this book, I use Roman numerals I, II, and III. These pages simply capsize the book of Revelation. However, you will not fully grasp an overall and clear understanding of the book of Revelation until you have completely read the verse-by-verse Commentary.

Let's start in the Old Testament where the **END reveals itself** through God's Prophets. These writings reveal much concerning our Savior's first visit and His next visit regarding the End Times. The revelations that God left behind are there to warn us, educate us, and enlighten us. This is a verse that encompasses the 1st and 2nd Coming of The Messiah. Let's start by looking at the Prophecy of **Daniel 9:24** *Seventy weeks are determined upon thy people and upon thy holy city, to finish the transgression, and to make an end of sins, and to make reconciliation for iniquity, and to bring in everlasting righteousness, and to seal up the vision and prophecy, and to anoint the most Holy.* **There are seven important aspects revealed in THIS ONE VERSE.** This brings to light the 1st and the 2nd Coming of Christ. ***Seventy weeks are determined upon thy people and upon thy holy city.*** The Hebrew word for *"week"* is *"shabuim"*. This means *"sevens"* of years. **Therefore 7 weeks equals 7 years**. Then, 69 of these 70 weeks of years or 483 years have already passed. This relates to the 1st coming of Christ over two thousand years ago. However, ONE *"week"* or the final seven years of this prophecy has yet to be fulfilled. Where is this missing week or 7 years of prophecy? This timeline does not follow chronologically the last *7 weeks* of *years,* **at this time, we are now in the "Church Age" aka the Age of Grace.** Many before me have worked through this timeline concluding the same. According to the Jewish year of 360 days, which gives us 483 years or 69 *"sevens"*; that day *(69th week)* Jesus entered Jerusalem on a donkey as The Messiah, *(Passover week)* as predicted by Daniel. After that 69th week, there was a time break between the 69th week and the 70th week, according to the prophecy. Then two colossal events took place. **First, was the Crucifixion of Jesus bringing Salvation to His Elect. Second, the destruction of Jerusalem in 70 AD**. Now some of this passage has been fulfilled at Christ's 1st Coming. The balance of this prophecy will be completed upon His 2nd Coming.

Let's continue to break it all down and unpack it one line at a time, ***to finish the transgression,*** is aimed at Israel's apostasy to bring an end to Israel's history of rebellion against God. This won't happen in full until the 2nd Coming, ***to make an end of sins,*** Jesus died on the cross once, for all death and sins of His Elect; past, present, and future. Next, ***to make reconciliation for iniquity,*** through a Transformation, *(being Born Again)* through Christ. This happened for Jews and Gentiles. However, **Salvation will ALSO come to The Nation of Israel on the day of the 2nd Coming**. Let's now visit **Zechariah 12:10 LSB** *And I will pour out on the house of David and on the inhabitants of Jerusalem the Spirit of grace and of supplication, so that they will look on Me* ***whom they have pierced****; and they will mourn for Him, as one mourns for an only son, and they will weep bitterly over Him like the bitter weeping over a firstborn.* **This happens at His 2nd Coming; Israel will weep and be drawn to Christ.** Furthermore, if you have ever visited Israel, they are totally against Jesus, the New Testament, and His Gospel. Indeed, today Israel is still under a Divine curse, rejecting Jesus.

Let's continue to unpack the verse of **Daniel 9:24.** These last three prophecies will happen at His 2nd Coming; ***to bring in everlasting righteousness,*** this refers to the return of Jesus as He establishes His Kingdom. The meaning of, ***to seal up the vision and prophecy***, brings the whole 66 books to vindication including the binding of Satan. Lastly, ***to anoint the most Holy***, refers to Jesus Christ our Messiah in the future Millennial Temple. This will be built before His Millennial Reign. This will all come together shortly.

The stage for Jesus' 2nd Coming was set through God's Providence before the Creation of this world. Indeed, before His first arrival as a baby; He is God incarnate. He was physically born from a virgin. He lived a sinless life to suffer and die on the Cross at Calvary, to rise from the dead on the third day. Therefore, defeating death *(death of death)* for all those His Father gave Him. Let's refer to **John 6:37-39** *(37) All that the Father giveth me shall come to me; and him that cometh to me I will in no wise cast out. (38) For I came down from heaven, not to do mine own will, but the will of him that sent me. (39) And this is the* ***Father's will*** *which hath sent me, that of* ***all which he <u>hath</u>***

given me* I should lose nothing** *but should raise it up again at the last day.* This is the Body of Christ, **those who are and will be Saved, the ones who live for Jesus to Glorify His Father through Him; God's Elect.** There is a huge transformation in those who die to themselves. They all will embrace Jesus as their Savior *(Redeemer).* They will obey ALL of His Word. Certainly, knowing their Salvation had or has or will have nothing to do with themselves at all. In conclusion, they each understand it has everything to do with God's process of Election, His Grace, His Mercy, and **NOT** your will but **HIS**. Let's look at **John 1:12-13 NASB** *(12) But as many as received Him, to them He gave the right to become children of God, to those who believe in His name, (13) who were born, not of blood, nor of the will of the flesh, nor of the will of a man, but of God.* **Salvation is all GOD'S WILL, period.** Remember this, Salvation is and will always be 100% God and 0% man. My 5th book ***"Digging Deeper into God's Truth Defines a Christian" addresses; Soteriology, Election, Depravity, Grace, and what "Born

Again" truly means. If you haven't read that book yet, please get a copy. It's available online everywhere and also on my website. If you do not fully understand or are against **God's Sovereignty** through His Election Process, then you will be determined and tempted to twist scripture throughout the Bible constantly. **It's vital that you fully understand the Doctrines of Election and the Doctrines of Depravity.** This will allow you to understand the doctrines of God's Grace. The Book of Revelation will not make sense to those who cannot first comprehend these doctrines. **All Believers make a <u>Profession</u> of faith *(even false converts)*. What truly matters is the <u>Possession</u> of Faith; the Big Difference is that one is initiated by oneself, the other by GOD Himself.** We must learn to be consistent with doctrinal truths. **There should be NO reluctance for any True Believer, in becoming a more mature Believer. Amen.** I sincerely hope that you look forward to completing your reading of this book, *"Examine The End Times"*. There is a Blessing waiting. Let's jump now to

Daniel 9:27 *And* ***he*** *shall confirm the covenant with many for one week: and in the midst of the week he shall cause the sacrifice and the oblation to cease, and for the overspreading of abominations he shall make it desolate, even until the consummation, and that determined shall be poured upon the desolate.* Let's break down this part of the prophecy. This is the future prediction of the final seven-year period aka the 70th week in the future. **This concerns the missing seven years,** *And he shall confirm;* The "he" is referring to the coming **Antichrist**. He will be everything Christ is not. He will be anti *(against)* Christ and motivated by Satan.

Furthermore, he will make peace with Israel during this time, making a 7-year pact; **a Covenant with Israel. The world will embrace him as a one-world global leader.** He will establish a one-world government, aka New World Order *(NWO).* He will use words like equity, equality, inclusion, environmental concerns, climate change, and taxes. He will be using gender-neutral pronouns concerning gender diversity, and he will approve open borders. The Antichrist will have online control of everyone's finances, creating one global economy. This uniformity will bring us into the one-world order. **The Antichrist will usher in this new world order as a world dictator**. He will desire full control using *(Marxism, liberalism, Fascism, Socialism, Progressivism, and Communism).* These are his signposts and he will accomplish his full agenda. **He will make his victims willingly comply through his slick persuasive speech, false propaganda, and Fake News. He will be yet another corrupt radical left lunatic.** The Antichrist will have control of the World Health Organization *(WHO),* World Economic Forum *(WEF), CDC, FDA*, *USAID, NATO*, *NIAID,* and the United Nations etc. He will have full control of the educational system. He will implement a liberal hate with a "woke" and homosexual agenda. He will use *(AI) surveillance* and be able to monitor everyone's cell phones and computers. The only news you will hear are liberal lies to fulfill his Godless agenda. This deceitful process of **government control** *(deep state)* has already begun, worldwide.

The Antichrist will seem to be a hero to many; a Convincing man, presiding over an evil Godless governmental organization. **We see the "birth pains" of the "End Times" even today. It's coming to fruition in today's democratic party.** The Antichrist will have great influence for the first 3 ½ years and great fame. He will be well respected by most. He may be a liberal military leader but certainly a charismatic liberal pathological liar. He will have little regard for women and will be a homosexual, *(Daniel 11:37).* He will magnify himself above all. There is already a *One World Flag.* **This will be the start of the 7 years of Tribulation.** However, this *(one world order concept)* was attempted once back in **Genesis 11:1, 9,** *(1) And the whole earth was of one language, and of one speech.* Long story short, God did not allow this. **They were rebellious, prideful, and defiant to God;** ***sound familiar?*** Therefore, God confused their languages and He forced them to scatter. Their fiasco of uniting to build a tower to reach Heaven; is called the Tower of Babel. *(9) Therefore, is the name of it called Babel; because the Lord did there confound the language of all the earth: and from thence did the Lord scatter them abroad upon the face of all the earth.*

Let's turn **back to Daniel 9:27** *And in the midst of the week he shall cause the sacrifice and the oblation to cease;* This means he ***(the Antichrist)*** will break his Covenant, his pledge with Israel. This is **midway, 3 ½ years** into the 7 years of Tribulation, *and for the overspreading of abominations he shall make it desolate.* This means The Antichrist will cause great abominations against the Jews and what they hold sacred. He will then openly claim to be god, total Blasphemy.

Here Jesus speaks of this very time in **Matthew 24:21 LSB** *For then there will be a great tribulation, such as has not occurred since the beginning of the world until now, nor ever will.* This is what the Bible refers to as

Divine Wrath. **The Great Tribulation will happen concerning the last 3 ½ years of the seven years of "The Tribulation".** The world leader at this future time will be The Antichrist. He was prophesied and referred to in **Daniel 7:8** as **"Little Horn"** and in **Revelation 13:4-5** as **"The Beast"** aka **The Antichrist**. He will be a worldly charismatic liberal *(Democratic)* politician and **a talented professional liar working under the authority and power of Satan.** He will gain immense and full political domination and control, worldwide.

Let's get back to unpacking the **last part of Daniel 9:27** *even until the consummation, and that determined shall be poured upon the desolate.* His evil dictatorship will be poured out continuously. This will last until **The 2nd Coming,** that day will be a Day of Wrath, Trouble, Doom, and Distress. **It will come at the END of the 7 years of Tribulation.** The book of Revelation is written in chronological order and has real order to it. Moreover, much of it is written quite literally. Then again, other parts are written figuratively, and paradoxically, using imagery and metaphors. In **Daniel 9:24 gives us a capsized view of the predicted Birth of Christ and the start and end of the future 7-year Tribulation.** Now, where are God's Elect, *His Bride, His Church (Christ's body of Believers)* during that time? It will now become even more and more interesting! The word **Revelation** is derived from the Latin word meaning to **reveal or unveil** that which was hidden. All books of the Bible have to be understood using the principles of **Hermeneutics**, which define what is being said or written. We must use the **Bible to interpret the Bible**. All Scripture has an intended meaning. Therefore, scripture has <u>one correct interpretation</u>, while it may have countless applications. We must consider all the surrounding verses and chapters, while given the linguistic context of the **original language**. Then taking into account the **historical** and **cultural** meanings as well. Lastly, taking into consideration **WHO** each book or chapter of the Bible was written to. **No verse in the Bible should EVER be interpreted to contradict another verse or**

the overall message. We must use Exegesis "To Lead Out" from scripture, the original meaning; this is called exegetical teaching. This means we must use a serious *(real, correct)* interpretation *(truth)* of a verse. **We never want to use Eisegesis** which means to **"Read Into"** scripture, your particular meanings. This practice is used worldwide by false teachers and false pastors. Indeed, many are Spiritually and theologically illiterate. What many "pastors" do is use verses that do not refer to the subject at hand. They may seem to "fit" and one can be easily bamboozled. **When one is confronted with an unclear verse, we find a clear verse to help interpret it correctly.** What I have explained so far is that the Bible does interpret itself. However, it is essential to have **a decent working knowledge and a good understanding of the first 65 books to truly understand the last book**. The Book of Revelation, the 66th Book will go from one verse referring to Earth then another verse concerning Heaven. Some passages must be cross-referenced using the Old & New Testaments. **They must be harmonized**

to confirm a better understanding of this last Book. Let's turn to **1 Corinthians 2:14** *But the natural man receiveth not the things of the Spirit of God: for they are foolishness unto him: neither can he know them, because they are spiritually discerned.* Let's unpack this very important verse. **There is no way the world can understand Spiritual things**. The Bible is a Spiritual Book. First of all, one cannot "convert" to Christianity; one must be Born Again by God *(to have an ear to hear and an eye to see).* When this verse speaks of the "natural man" this means the unconverted, unredeemed person. **This is or was the condition of each of us.** Let's turn to **2 Peter 1:20 ESV** *knowing this first of all, that no prophecy of Scripture comes from someone's own interpretation.* This means All Scripture is God-breathed. **Yet, one verse at a time, the Commentary may open your eyes to His Truths, keep reading...**

"The Bible cannot be understood simply by study or talent, you must count only on the influence of the Holy Spirit."

Martin Luther, *Theologian - Reformer*

II

What Time is It?

People are always asking, "Are we living in the End Times"? In a way, yes, and in a way no. **Everything that has taken place after the ascension of Jesus takes place in what the Bible refers to as The End Times.** We are still in the end times as I write *"EXAMINE THE END TIMES"* as stated in The New Testament. Let's turn to **Hebrews 1:1-2 LSB** *(1) God, having spoken long ago to the fathers in the prophets in many portions and in many ways, (2) in* ***these last days*** *spoke to us in His Son, whom He appointed heir of all things, through whom also He made the worlds,* **The last days started when Jesus ascended back to Heaven.**

Let's look at **Matthew 24:14** *And this gospel of the kingdom shall be preached in all the world for a witness unto all nations; and then shall the end come*. Jesus was referring to a time when all of the whole world would hear and know of His Gospel. This time has already arrived. We have the completed Bible, Modern Technology, Books, TV, Radio, and the Internet. God's Truths are available to everyone worldwide. If you are asking, are we at the END, of the "end times" as taught in the last book of the Bible, the Book of Revelation? **No, we are in a time of God's GRACE.** Today's *time* is **before** The Tribulation period starts. The next thing to happen Biblically and Prophetically is that Jesus will come, ***(The Rapture)***. **We are close because everything God HATES is being "normalized".** If we speak up against it, the world persecutes us. Today, sin is applauded and Christianity is condemned. These are the ***Birth Pains of the Rapture*** *(Pages 158-163, 197-200)*. Look at **Isaiah 5:20** *Woe unto them that* ***call evil good, and good evil;*** *and put darkness for light, and light for darkness...* **Sound familiar?**

Let's look at **1 Thessalonians 4:16-17** *(16) "For the Lord himself shall descend from heaven with a shout, with the voice of the archangel, and with the trump of God: and the dead in Christ shall rise first:" (17) "Then we* *which are alive and remain shall be caught up together with them in the clouds, to meet the Lord in the air: and so shall we ever be with the Lord."* Let me unpack these two verses. JESUS HIMSELF will come to Earth. He will NOT touch down ***(this is NOT the 2nd Coming)!*** He will use HIS voice as in a Shout, a Command of infinite authority! He will meet His Elect, His Bride, aka **His Church** *(body of Believers)* in the air. We *shall be 'caught up' together.* This word is a Latin verb *(rapio)* that means to "seize" or "to carry off violently". The Greek word *'harpazo'* means to grasp hastily, lift, or Rapture. In the Latin, Vulgate, it is *"rapturo".* I will use the word **Rapture** in this book. This will be a meeting in the air with the Lord Himself. "*With the trump of God: and the dead in Christ shall rise first:"* This Trumpet of God is not to be confused with the Judgment Trumpets. This will be more like a Trumpet of Deliverance and Triumph, a sound we as Believers only hear! Perhaps, Jesus' own voice as in **Revelation 1:10** when John heard a great voice of a trumpet, and it was Jesus! Let's now visit, **1 Corinthians 15:52** *In a moment,* *in the twinkling of an eye, at the last trump: for the trumpet shall sound, and the dead shall be raised incorruptible, and we shall be changed.* This is talking about The Rapture.

Let's go back to unpacking even deeper, 1 Thessalonians 4:16. **This is a call for those IN CHRIST both dead and alive to assemble.** When it says; "*and the dead* ***in Christ*** *shall rise first:*" This means all the bones, bodies, ashes and all the *(remains)* of those **who died In Christ** in the past will rise first. This will be from their coffins, the sea, their graves, and their ashes in the air, for God nothing is impossible. **Their spirits are already in Heaven.** This refers to a New Glorified Body that each Believer will receive. Moments after that, all the living Believers *(His, Church)* will be taken away. The spirits *(souls)* of the dead *(those who died before the Rapture)* **In Christ**, are already with The Lord. Let's see **2 Corinthians 5:8** *We are confident, I say, and willing rather to be absent from the body, and to be present with the Lord.* This means when a Born Again by God Believer dies, their Spirit goes straight to Heaven. Let's look at **Philippians 1:23 LSB** *But I am hard-pressed between the two, having the desire to depart and be with Christ, for that is very much better.* We see the Apostle Paul clearing this issue up. When one is **IN CHRIST** and dies, it's imminent and immediate that their souls go to Heaven, straight away.

Now back to unpack **1 Thessalonians 4:17** *"Then we which are alive and remain shall be caught up together with them in the clouds, to meet the Lord in the air: and so shall we ever be with the Lord."* This verse says that those who are on Earth, those who are of God's Elect *(His Church)* will be caught up. We will be taken and snatched away right after the dead bodies **In Christ** are taken. The True Christians alive at that time will be Raptured (taken up). Then they will all immediately receive new *Glorified Bodies* and will forever be with The Lord! Moreover, this all happens in a blink of an eye! What an Infinitely Powerful GOD we serve! There are drastic differences in verses used in the Bible that describe Christ coming in

Judgment. Those verses concern, The 2nd Coming. This **is the Rapture**; **NOT** The 2nd Coming. The next two verses also confirm the Rapture. Let's turn to **Revelation 3:10 NASB** *Because you have kept My word of perseverance, I also will keep you from the <u>hour of the testing</u>, that hour which is about to come <u>upon the whole world</u>, to test those who live on the earth.* Jesus says He will keep His Elect; they will be Saved from going through the *(hour of testing)*, which is the horror of The Tribulation. This further supports the **Pre-tribulation Rapture**. *I will later address all alternate views, (Types of Beliefs, Pages 266-273).* **If you have children and they're outside playing and you know a great and dangerous storm is coming; will you call them to come home? God calls His Own Children, His *(Elect)* to come Home.**

Let's turn to **John 14:3 LSB** *And if I go and prepare a place for you, I will come again and receive you to Myself, that where I am, there you may be also.* Jesus is saying He will return to gather His Own to Him. **This is not**

Him coming in Judgment but to remove His Church. Therefore, the **Rapture is pre-tribulation**, meaning it happens **before** the 7 years of Tribulation. **The 2nd Coming** happens **after** the 7 years of Tribulation. The Church *(God's Elect)* will be in Heaven. It will become clearer very soon *(Pages 276-279)*.

Let's turn now to **Revelation 4:10-11** *The <u>four and twenty elders</u> fall down before him that sat on the throne, and worship him that liveth for ever and ever, and cast their crowns before the throne....* The 24 Elders signify **The Church**, in Heaven. In Revelation chapters 2-3 we see Christians there. The Church is mentioned 19 times. In Revelation chapters 4-5 the Christians; the "Church" have gone, they will have been Raptured. Revelation chapters 6-18 there is complete wickedness on Earth. Revelation chapter 19 Jesus returns. In chapter 20 Jesus sets up His 1000-year reign in Jerusalem. In chapters 20-22 a New Heaven and New Earth. **It will all be broken down soon, in a way that the average "Joe" will understand.**

III

Overview of END TIMES

Let's turn to **Matthew 24:1-3 LSB** *(1) And coming out from the temple, Jesus was going along, and His disciples came up to point out the temple buildings to Him. (2) And He answered and said to them, "Do you not see all these things? Truly I say to you, not one stone here will be left upon another, which will not be torn down."* History tells us in the year 70 AD the Roman Army destroyed Jerusalem and the Temple. They **left no stone walls standing** and 1.1 million Jews were killed. *(3) Now as He (Jesus) was sitting on the Mount of Olives, the disciples came to Him privately, saying, "Tell us, when will these things happen, and what will be the sign of Your coming and of the end of the age?"* Jesus spoke about the walls coming down and then jumped to the start of the end, The Tribulation. Let's turn to **Matthew 24:4-14 LSB** *(4) And Jesus answered and said to them, See to it that* ***no one deceives you.*** Today we have **deceit** from TBN and other false faith-based networks. Then, Fake News networks *(Leftist)* e.g. CNN, ABC, NBC, CBS, MSNBC, and others, knowingly in cahoots report the same exact fabricated talking points! Then let's add the sinful intentional brainwashing and salacious lies, the Grooming and ongoing Sexualization of children by mainstream media, schools, social media, Hollywood, and even Disney! In addition to that list, the countless pedophiles, phony televangelists, and counterfeit pastors. *(5) For many will come in My name, saying, 'I am the Christ,' and will deceive many.* This is happening all over, just ask any online search engine. *(6) And you are going to hear of wars and rumors of wars. See that you are not alarmed, for those things must take place, but that is not yet the end.* Turn on any reputable News Station. *(7) For nation will rise against nation, and kingdom against kingdom, and in various places there will be famines and earthquakes.* Again, turn on any reputable News Station. *(8) But all these things are merely the* ***beginning of birth pains****. (9) Then they will deliver you to tribulation, and* *will* ***kill you****, and* ***you will be hated*** *by all nations because of My name.* This is happening all over the world, in all Islamic Muslim countries, including China, India, Iran, North Korea, Pakistan, Russia, Saudi Arabia, Syria, and Vietnam. Indeed, many are being killed each day because of their Faith **In Christ**! There are many days when I and countless other Christians are unfairly hated and ostracized. We are treated as outcasts by strangers, friends, family, and false converts. However, when I dwell on that, I must move to remember that **I am also unfairly loved by God.** Furthermore, we MUST focus on Him *(Jesus)* not ourselves. *(10) And at that time many will fall away and will betray one another and hate one another.* There are countless Christians who fall away daily. **They were never Born Again by God but deceived by their OWN selfish, self-centered, free will.** These false converts will **HATE YOU** and even grow to hate the Truth in you. *(11) Many false prophets will arise and will deceive many.* Today there are countless false teachers, false preachers, two-faced greedy televangelists, and **false**

converts, everywhere! Additionally, all those claiming today to be a *"Prophet or Apostle"* are false. Line them up... *(12) And because lawlessness is multiplied, most people's love will grow cold.* All True Christians MUST VOTE and vote conservatively. **Ecclesiastes 10:2** *A wise man's heart is at his right hand; but a fool's heart at his left.* Today there are countless fake "Christians" *(false converts).* A small window to one's heart is through voting. Countless fake "Christians" vote for liberal politicians and their wicked & perverted platforms. They vote for laws of corruption and **even try to imprison their political opponents!** This is today's American democratic/socialist platform. Yet, many dare to call themselves a "Christian". *(13) But the one who endures to the end, he will be saved.* Jesus is stating that those who are HIS will remain His. This means throughout any hardships we will remain constant in our Faith; such are His Elect. God's Elect will grow in Sanctification daily through our faults and failures and as a result, become more Christ-like each day. **Consequently,**

the Words of God mean more to us *(Elect)* than the words of people. God does NOT un-adopt those Born Again by Him. **His Adoption is for eternity.** *(14) And this gospel of the kingdom shall be proclaimed in the whole world as a witness to all the nations, and then the end will come.* **This time has arrived. There are now mass communications with social media and the internet, worldwide. This brings us to the fact that Jesus can come at any time to gather His Elect, even today.** Believers are ***The Watchmen*** who must warn all others of what's to come. The "Church" will be removed before The Tribulation. However, God does choose to quicken the hearts of some of His Elect during the 7 years of The Tribulation. **The main difference between the *Rapture* of The Church and the 2nd *Coming*** of Jesus is 7 years. The Rapture is an isolated event. I dare say a private event that happens in the twinkling of an eye *(instantaneous)* and is ONLY for God's Church *(Elect)*. There will be no one who will be able to witness it, only the devastating after-effects. The Elect, aka *The Church,* are meeting Jesus **in the air** and **are going up**. The 2nd Coming involves The Wrath of Jesus concerning the unredeemed, the Deliverance for Israel and Salvation for The Tribulation Saints. This will all happen at the end of the 7 years of Tribulation, at that time **Jesus will come down** from Heaven with His Armies of Heaven. This 2nd Coming of Jesus will be a public appearance that the whole world will witness. Let's turn to **Revelation 1:7 LSB** *Behold, He is coming with the clouds, and every eye will see Him, even those who pierced Him; and all the tribes of the earth will mourn over Him. Yes, amen.* Jesus will put down His enemies and set up His Kingdom. The first time He came as a Lamb to save many of sin. **The 2nd Coming will be in His Wrath, as a LION for War, Righteousness, Justice, and to Punish sinners. Throughout scripture, God uses Sheep when He describes or speaks of His Elect, then He uses goats when He speaks of the *(unredeemed)*, lost**. These verses speak of what will happen on Judgment Day, after God's Millennial Reign. Let's look at **Matthew 25:32-33**, *(32) And before him*

(Jesus) shall be gathered all nations: and he shall separate them one from another, as a shepherd divideth his ***sheep from the goats****: (33) And he shall set* *the sheep on his right hand, but the goats on the left.* The Sheep will always remain Sheep, a goat never turns into a sheep and a sheep will never turn into a goat. **Some people are pre-elect Sheep. This means they were Born *Elect* but God has not *quickened* their hearts as of yet.** This means they are still blind to Him and His Truths until He wants them to see. **This could be YOU today...**

Let's turn to **Ephesians 1:4-5 LSB** *(4) just as He chose us (Elect) in Him before the foundation of the world, that we (Elect) would be holy and blameless before Him in love, (5) by predestining us (Elect) to adoption as sons through Jesus Christ to Himself, according to the good pleasure of* ***His will.*** There is no way of knowing for sure if or when God will convert a dead soul. **The Book of Life** was written **before** the foundation of the world. Let's now turn to **Revelation 17:8 LSB** *The beast that you saw was, and is not, and is* *about to come up out of the abyss and go to destruction. And those who dwell on the earth, whose name has not been written in the book of life from the foundation of the world, will wonder when they see the beast, that he was and is not and will come.* This verse refers to the false resurrection of the Antichrist, who after he stages his false demise; a great demon will possess him from the abyss. We will get into that soon... The **Book of Life** has all the names of God's Elect, that GOD chose BEFORE the foundation of the world, in eternity past. There will be none lost. I have personally witnessed countless times when a false pastor or teacher would invite people up to his platform, altar, or ***stage***. Then he would say to them walk the aisle or raise your hand and then lead them into a *"sinner's prayer"*. Then he would pronounce them Saved. Lastly, he would tell them, "Your name was just written in the Book of Life" or "Welcome to the family"! Wow, such trickery, lies, and deceit. This is what "churches" today have become, breeding grounds for more and more false converts. **They create an**

artificial salvation called "easy believism" aka "free will" salvation. This is a false twisted watered-down gospel, selling a false jesus. Those who attend false "churches" are Not **In Christ**. It's God, giving *False Converts* what they truly desire, **not Him**. The "altar call" is Heresy nonsense which was started by Charles Finney in the 1800s. **It is still taught and practiced in gospel-illiterate "churches" today!** This is what today's phony "Christians" want, merely a surface appearance of Salvation. Fire Insurance...

> **"If your Christian conversion did not reverse the direction of your life, if it did not transform it then you are NOT converted at all. You are simply a victim of the 'Accept Jesus' HERESY!"**
>
> A. W. Tozer, *Pastor*

There will be no excuse for those who desire sin, over Him. Let's visit **Romans 1:18-22 LSB** *(18) For the wrath of* ***God is revealed*** *from heaven against all ungodliness and unrighteousness of men who* <u>*suppress the truth in unrighteousness*</u>*,* God's Wisdom and Wrath are made known and exposed throughout scripture. However, those who overturn His Truths are the unrighteous e.g. *Joel Osteen.* They go against God's standards and love sin more than God. *(19) because* ***that which is known about God is evident within them****; for God made it evident to them.* **In our cold hearts, we know moral right from wrong and choose WRONG.** *(20) For since the creation of the world His invisible attributes, both His eternal power and divine nature, have been clearly seen, being understood through what has been made, so that* ***they are without excuse****.* We all can look and realize this world was all God's Creation, not ours. There is ample evidence of Him. *(21) For <u>even though they knew God</u>, they did not glorify Him as God or give thanks, but they became futile in their thoughts, and their foolish heart was darkened.* This says even those who claim to KNOW HIM did what's right in their own eyes! They rejected God and *(Jesus).* Their SIN and faults have a cause and effect. **The national anthem in Hell is "I DID IT MY WAY".** God then gives them up to a reprobate mind and false teachers. He then allows their insane wickedness which leads to their own sinful demise. **Don't harden your heart for Him. Don't be slow to believe; all of God's Truths MATTER!** *(22) Professing to be wise, they* ***became fools,*** This is the state of mankind, always wanting their way. They disrespect God and are **NOT thankful for the Grace He gives daily.** Those who think themselves wise, God calls them fools. **TRUTH sounds like HATE to those who hate the truth.** Believers are the **Salt** and **Light** of this wicked world. When Jesus calls us Home or Returns before then, we want to be caught doing His Bidding, not ours. Live **In Christ** & die to oneself...

> **"God is not asking us to 'clean up' our lives; He is Commanding us to lay down our lives, for Him."**
>
> Joseph Malara, *Theologian*

> ***The 7-Year TRIBULATION will NOT begin before God's Elect (Bride, Church) leave the Earth***

Chapter 1

Commentary *Revelation Chapter 1*

In Rev. 1:1 *(1) The Revelation of Jesus Christ, which God gave unto him, to shew unto his servants things which must shortly come to pass; and he sent and signified it by his angel unto his servant John:* We see that **Father God** has originated this *Revelation.* He gave it **to Jesus** and Jesus gave it to **His angel**, who gave it to The **Apostle John**, who while in The Spirit gave it to **us** all in writing.

In Rev. 1:2 *(2) Who bare record of the word of God, and of the testimony of Jesus Christ, and of all things that he saw.* The Apostle John was given a "live vision" as if he was personally there. **He is watching and witnessing such future events seemingly in real-time.**

In Rev. 1:3 *(3) Blessed is he that readeth, and they that hear the words of this prophecy, and keep those things which are written therein: for the* ***time is at hand***. This is the only book in the 66 Books of The Bible that gives this promise by God, that whoever reads and KEEPS the things written therein will be blessed. **This gives us a true motivation to live a life of obedience which is pleasing to God.** We can do this by studying, meditating, learning, and applying His written Word to our daily lives. Look at **James 1:22** *But be ye* ***doers of the word, and not hearers only, deceiving your own selves.*** David defeated Goliath but lost to Bathsheba, our desires must turn to God.

In Rev. 1:4 *(4) John to the seven churches which are in Asia: Grace be unto you, and peace, from him which is, and which was, and which is to come; and from the seven Spirits which are before his throne;* The Apostle John was to give each of the seven churches that John understood at that time, this Book The Revelation of Jesus. Furthermore, such descriptions and dire warnings in it certainly apply to us even today.

In Rev. 1:5 *(5) And from Jesus Christ, who is the faithful witness, and the first* *begotten of the dead, and the prince of the kings of the earth. Unto him that loved us, and washed us from our sins in his own blood,* Jesus was the first to rise from the dead. He is the King of Kings and the Savior of His Redeemed *(Elect).*

In Rev. 1:6 *(6) And hath made us kings and priests unto God and his Father; to him be glory and dominion for ever and ever. Amen.* All Born Again by God Believers are priests *(ministers).* We live to bring Glory to the Father through His Son Jesus Christ. Namely, by obeying His written Word. This includes The Great Commission, telling all we know of Him; **being a Christian is bold, revealing, and always public**.

In Rev. 1:7 *(7) Behold, he cometh with clouds; and every eye shall see him, and they also which pierced him: and all kindreds of the earth shall wail because of him. Even so, Amen.* This is speaking as a reference to the Jews *(Israelites).* They were partly responsible for His death. This is also speaking of the **2nd Coming** and **not** The Rapture because here every eye will see Him.

In Rev. 1:8 *(8) I am Alpha and Omega, the beginning and the ending, saith the Lord, which is, and which was, and which is to come, the Almighty.* It is all about Jesus. He is The Alpha and Omega. He has Sovereign control over every person, everything and every event. Furthermore, nothing is outside of His Will. Also, before the book entitled "The Revelation" we only had part of God's Plan. Now, we have the rest of what He wants us to know. This way we can learn from it, then teach others, warn others, and prepare for His Return as well. This book takes off the veil so we can better understand Christ in His Fullness, Divinity and what the future unquestionably holds. **He will make all things happen, just as written.**

In Rev. 1:9 *(9) I John, who also am your brother, and companion in tribulation, and in the kingdom and patience of Jesus Christ, was in the isle that is called Patmos, for the word of God, and for the testimony of Jesus*

Christ. We read that during the Apostle John's life, he suffered greatly for Christ. He is not talking here of "The Tribulation" but tribulation itself. John was exiled to the small island of Patmos as a punishment for preaching the gospel of Jesus. **If you're not going through alienation, if you're not being ostracized by friends and family because of Christ in you; maybe He is not.**

Now turn to **Romans 8:18** *For I reckon that the* ***sufferings of this present time*** *are not worthy to be compared with the glory which shall be revealed in us.* Look now at **Luke 6:26** ***Woe unto you, when all men shall speak well of you! for so did their fathers to the false prophets.*** When professing His Truths; you will be **hated**, not loved. **However, False converts are loved by many.**

In Rev. 1:10 *(10) I was in the Spirit on the Lord's Day, and heard behind me a great voice, as of a trumpet.* This is not to be confused with "The Day of The Lord" which is His 2nd Coming. This here means the

Sunday of His Resurrection. The first day of the week is Sunday. The Apostle John was in the Spirit, and he was supernaturally taken to see all God wanted him to see.

In Rev. 1:11 *(11) Saying, I am Alpha and Omega, the first and the last: and, What thou seest, write in a book, and send it unto the seven churches which are in Asia; unto Ephesus, and unto Smyrna, and unto Pergamos, and unto Thyatira, and unto Sardis, and unto Philadelphia, and unto Laodicea.* Jesus is speaking to the Apostle John. Jesus told John that He is the Alpha and Omega, **the beginning and the end**. He Commands the Apostle John to write down all he sees and send it to the seven churches.

In Rev. 1:12 *(12) And I turned to see the voice that spake with me. And being turned, I saw seven golden candlesticks;* The Apostle John turned to see **who** was speaking, it was **The Lord of Lords *(Jesus)* Himself!**

In Rev. 1:13 *(13) And in the midst of the seven candlesticks one like unto the Son of man, clothed with a garment down to the foot,* *and girt about the paps with a golden girdle.* **The seven candlesticks are the seven churches. The Son of Man is Jesus.**

In Rev 1:14 *(14) His head and his hairs were white like wool, as white as snow; and his eyes were as a flame of fire;* Jesus is all Glory and His appearance indescribable. The Apostle attempts to describe the indescribable. His eyes are like piercing fire able to discern and judge all things at the same time. Hair white with infinite wisdom and glowing with Holy Glory.

In Rev. 1:15 *(15) And his feet like unto fine brass, as if they burned in a furnace; and his voice as the sound of many waters.* This is the best The Apostle could do in mere words to explain the unexplainable. The words speak for themselves. His voice was like many waters exhibiting great strength, wisdom, respect, and authority. **He is The Word of Life, the voice of all things that were, are, and will be. Wow!**

In Rev. 1:16 *(16) And he had in his right hand seven stars: and out of his mouth* *went a sharp two-edged sword: and his countenance was as the sun shineth in his strength.* The seven stars are the seven messengers *(angels)* to the churches. The Word's from His mouth create all things and permanently judges all things. He has unthinkable and immeasurable power.

In Rev. 1:17 *(17) And when I saw him, I fell at his feet as dead. And he laid his right hand upon me, saying unto me, Fear not; I am the first and the last:* When the Apostle John **sees His Lord in Heaven he will fall at His feet as dead**. The Apostle John knew and loved Jesus personally! I have run into many who have told me, "When I see God I am going to tell Him this or that!" The truth is when anyone sees God, they will fall on their face speechless, teary-eyed, and trembling with great, great fear! Rightly so...

In Rev. 1:18 LSB *(18) and the living One; and I was dead, and behold, I am alive forever and ever, and I have the keys of death and of Hades.* This verse tells us that Jesus has power over Life and Death. "Hades" is the Greek word for the unseen world. It means more than the grave where a body lies, it's a place where the spirit goes. I explain this in the book ***"Digging Deeper into God's Truth Defines a Christian".***

In Rev. 1:19 *(19) Write the things which thou hast seen, and the things which are, and the things which shall be hereafter;* Jesus is commanding the Apostle John to write.

In Rev. 1:20 *(20) The mystery of the seven stars which thou sawest in my right hand, and the seven golden candlesticks. The* ***seven stars are the angels of the seven churches: and the seven candlesticks which thou sawest are the seven churches***. There were seven heads *(messengers, elders, pastors)* of the seven churches and an *angel* will **make certain** this book gets to each church.

"The Bible is alive, it speaks to me; it has feet, it runs after me, it has hands, it lays hold of me."

Martin Luther, *Theologian - Reformer*

Chapter 2

Commentary *Revelation Chapter 2*

In Rev. 2:1 *(1) Unto the angel of the* ***Church of Ephesus*** *write; These things saith he that holdeth the seven stars in his right hand, who walketh in the midst of the seven golden candlesticks;* This letter *(Revelation)* is to be given to the elder or pastor of each of the seven churches. **This means that an *angel* would make a way of <u>certainty</u> that John's letter was received by all those God Commanded.**

This message was to seven real churches of the first and second centuries, some into the third century. These "churches" that Jesus speaks of were in existence during the Church Age. **The *Church Age* started when Christ ascended into Heaven. It continues today as I write this book. It will end at the *Rapture*.** The assessment you will read of Jesus's evaluations and Judgments also reflects the "churches" of today and is relevant. We can use such wisdom from God to expose today's false "churches" and we must!

In Rev. 2:2 *(2) I know thy works, and thy labour, and thy patience, and how thou canst not bear them which are evil: and thou hast tried them which say they are apostles, and are not, and hast found them liars:* Jesus is Truth; He Hates Evil and all those who lie. He commands and then rebukes. He exposes the false apostles *(pastors)* and churches. **He will judge rigorously, righteously, and conclusively.**

In Rev. 2:3 *(3) And hast borne, and hast patience, and for my name's sake hast laboured, and hast not fainted.* This church **started well** and remained in God's Truths for a while.

In Rev. 2:4 *(4) Nevertheless I have somewhat against thee, because thou hast left thy first love.* We see why they started downward, **they lost their first love**, **HIM** and their zeal for God's Truths. Their continued Sanctification *(Spiritual growth)* became non-existent. This reveals a false conversion. **A "church" filled with *(lost)* unconverted members, playing "church".**

In Rev. 2:5 *(5) Remember therefore from whence thou art fallen, and repent, and do the first works; or else I will come unto thee quickly, and will remove thy candlestick out of his place, except thou repent.* Jesus knows they have fallen. When a "church" does so, it only gets worse. His Judgment moved to end this so-called "church".

In Rev. 2:6 *(6) But this thou hast, that thou hatest the deeds of the Nicolaitanes, which I also hate.* **They were apostates, false converts whom God Hated.** These "Christian" churches regularly supply **entertainment today**. **They don't use expository preaching *(verse-by-verse)* teaching.** They shy away from the doctrine of **Election** and the doctrine of **Depravity**. **There is no talk of SIN, HELL, or Repentance.** They say to bring your friends and let's grow together in Biblically watered-down and twisted scripture. This is all worldly nonsense! Beware! **There was a**

time when people went to church, heard the truth, and wept because of their sins. Now, people go to "church" hear a motivational speech, get entertained, overlook and promote their sins.

In Rev. 2:7 *(7) He that hath an ear, let him hear what the Spirit saith unto the churches; To him that overcometh will I give to eat of the tree of life, which is in the midst of the paradise of God.* This is a dire warning to all who read this, **be one who overcomes.**

Let's recap, the church of Ephesus. They left their first love, Jesus. This happens to many who don't read and study His Word each day. **God MUST be first**, before and over your spouse, kids, house, life, job, and oneself. He alone is worthy of all our worship, time, and praise, period.

If you feel content and stagnant in what you know of God today, then you are not growing in Sanctification and you don't know Jesus. Let's look at **Luke 8:13 LSB** *And those (Seeds) aka (Word of God) on the rock are those who, when they hear,* *receive the word with joy, and these have no root; they believe for a while, and in time of temptation fall away.* **This happens today to over 90% of all so-called believers, I was one...**But God.

> **"A 'church' that cannot grasp Biblical Truths must be entertained, and men who cannot lead a 'church' in God's Truths must provide continuous entertainment."**
>
> Joseph Malara, *Theologian*

In Rev. 2:8 *(8) And unto the angel of the* ***church in Smyrna*** *write; These things saith the first and the last, which was dead, and is alive;* This church was taught Biblical Truths by **Polycarp**. **He was a long-time friend and student of the Apostle John.**

In Rev. 2:9 *(9) I know thy works, and tribulation, and poverty, (but thou art rich) and I know the blasphemy of them which say they are Jews, and are not, but are the synagogue of Satan.* He knows those who are the pagans. Jesus moves on and speaks well on behalf of this church. He knows their suffering and says to remain faithful.

In Rev. 2:10 *(10) Fear none of those things which thou shalt suffer: behold, the devil shall cast some of you into prison, that ye may be tried; and ye shall have tribulation ten days: be thou faithful unto death, and I will give thee a crown of life.* This means that Jesus knows all of what we each go through for Him. **He says to be faithful unto death.** He says here, that He will give them the **Crown of Life**. This should be the type of "Church People" you must be. Whatever the case, stay strong through whatever life throws at you. Certainly, knowing that **Jesus sees and knows your pains for Him.** He will reward such in time; **rejoice** again rejoice!

In Rev. 2:11 *(11) He that hath an ear, let him hear what the Spirit saith unto the churches; He that overcometh shall not be hurt of the second death.* Again, Jesus dialogs to His Elect. He instructs them that the *second death* which is Judgment *(Hell)* will not be their situation.

Let's recap the church at Smyrna, Jesus speaks well and says to them to

remain faithful. He will give them each **the Crown of Life.**

In Rev. 2:12 *(12) And to the angel of the* ***church in Pergamos*** *write; These things saith he which hath the sharp sword with two edges;* Jesus proclaims His Words are indeed as sharp as a two-edged sword.

In Rev. 2:13 *(13) I know thy works, and where thou dwellest, even where Satan's seat is: and thou holdest fast my name, and hast not denied my faith, even in those days wherein Antipas was my faithful martyr, who was slain among you, where Satan dwelleth.* **We see here, that Jesus is speaking of pagan worship**. The place where Caesar was worshipped was a place where Satan dwelled. However, Antipas was *(faithful to Christ)* the son of *Herod the Great* who ruled during Christ's lifetime.

Jesus says this is where Satan's seat is, this means **a watered-down false Gospel**, a false doctrine of Christ such **a "church" uses His Name, but is spiritually DEAD**. This is describing about 90% of today's

"Christian Churches", some say 99%. **Today false churches are the ones where there is an alter call, an invitation to *"accept"*, "*choose"*, *"decide on"*, or *"give your life to Jesus"* which is Biblically impossible!** There will be soft music and a false *"pastor"* saying raise your hand, walk up to my stage or platform, and repeat after me. This is blasphemy to a Holy and Righteous God. Let's see **John 15:16** *Ye have* ***not*** *chosen me, but I have chosen you, and ordained you, that ye should go and bring forth fruit...* Father God Chooses His Son's Bride, not you and not me. It is all His Mercy and His Grace. **We only supply the sin that He died for...**

If you think YOU had something or ANYTHING to do with your salvation, you are greatly mistaken, or a false convert. I know, I was a false convert for over 20 years until God gave me sight. When I thought I was saved, **I was on fire for the Lord**. I had bumper stickers all over my car. I gave out Bible tracts and I led many in the "sinner's prayer", which is unbiblical. **I did great damage by leading others to believe they**

were saved, due to some prayer I had them repeat! I silently went back to the world, because I was in the world and of the world. Did you notice how many times I used the word **"I"**? I was bamboozled like many others are each day! However, 20 years later, due to **His** Doing, NOT MINE, His Mercy, and His Grace; I received His message loud and clear. **He gave me** True Salvation and as a result, a New Heart through Christ. I was then Born Again by HIM. **There is such a huge contrast between being a false convert and having your life transformed by GOD into a True Convert;** e.g., before being truly Born Again by GOD, I would have never denied Him, but **I was lost**. I viewed Jesus as a part of my life. **However, once Saved He became my life;** the difference between night and day, Heaven and Hell.

I knew a man when I was still a baby Christian, **he had Bible-written verses all over his entire car.** He even had clothes embroidered proclaiming *Jesus Saves.* I was talking to him about God's Election process one day, he didn't agree with it. He told me a story; he gave a certain guy a Bible tract and the man refused it. Then he told the man, "I thought you were smart, but I see you are not". This type of arrogance could NEVER come from a True Believer! It is never how "smart" someone is or isn't. **It's about God interceding and initiating Salvation in a heart.** It just so happened I was able to contact this old *"acquaintance"* on social media nineteen years later. He was very abusive, prideful, and insulting in his written approach to me. **Those we believe to be true converts are many times just good used car salesmen, selling a false jesus.** He showed **misguided good works** like those of this "church" in Pergamos. This serves as a reminder, that Salvation is NOT about any religious performance. **If ANYONE takes ANY credit for their salvation that would expose it as invalid, null, and void.**

> **"Just as you had nothing to do with your first birth, your physical birth, you will have nothing to do with your Spiritual Birth, It is a Divine work of God."**
>
> John MacArthur, *Pastor-Teacher*

> **"I have discovered that so few 'Christians' truly know, understand, or care to know ELECTION. This reflects the inaccurate and sad state of those collectively avoiding the full teaching of God's Word. This exposes the 'user-friendly churches', the 'entertainment churches', and the 'dead churches' and who they honestly are and who they truly represent, the misinformed and the lost."**
>
> Joseph Malara, *Theologian*

In Rev. 2:14 *(14) But I have a few things against thee, because thou hast there them that hold the doctrine of Balaam, who taught Balac to cast a stumblingblock before the children of Israel, to eat things sacrificed unto idols, and to commit fornication.* The Balaam doctrine *(The Book of Numbers)* encouraged the Israelites to worship idols.

In Rev. 2:15 *(15) So hast thou also them that hold the doctrine of the Nicolaitanes, **which thing I hate**.* This is to say that the Nicolaitans along with Balaam sanctioned eating things sacrificed to idols and there was also sexual immorality.

In Rev. 2:16 *(16) Repent; or else I will come unto thee quickly, and will fight against them with the sword of my mouth.* The words of Jesus *(sword of His mouth)* pronounce Righteous Judgment. Then He will carry out immediate Justice.

In Rev. 2:17 *(17) He that hath an ear, let him hear what the Spirit saith unto the churches; To him that overcometh will I give to eat of the hidden manna, and will give him a white stone, and in the stone a new name written, which no man knoweth saving he that receiveth it.* Then Jesus will bestow a personal honor *(tribute)* in Heaven to those who overcome adversity for His Name's sake. Only, God's Elect have an ear to hear.

Let's recap the church in Pergamos. We see, Jesus was not happy. They did tolerate false teaching, idolatry and were a worldly church. He moves to offer a *(tribute)* to those who overcome ***(leave such false teaching),*** I have... **These "churches" are *Social Clubs* and *Concert Halls* where people come to smile, hang out, serve**

coffee, listen to a tickling-the-ears sermonette, and clap at the live entertainment! This is NOT of God, but Satan.

In Rev. 2:18 *(18) And unto the angel of the* ***church in Thyatira*** *write; These things saith the Son of God, who hath his eyes like unto a flame of fire, and his feet are like fine brass;* Next, Jesus is described and speaks of the church in Thyatira. His eyes were all-knowing and **His Impervious Feet Have *Walked the Walk* of His Mighty Words!**

In Rev. 2:19 *(19) I know thy works, and charity, and service, and faith, and thy patience, and thy works; and the last to be more than the first.* **This church was not short of *(misguided)* good works.**

In Rev. 2:20 *(20) Notwithstanding I have a few things against thee, because thou sufferest that woman Jezebel, which calleth herself a prophetess, to teach and to seduce my servants to commit fornication, and to eat things sacrificed unto idols.* This church was a sure sign of **a perverted gospel**. Indeed, even women are involved, possibly behind a pulpit, a church full of sin. **This church era started by allowing the unconverted world into the church.** The True Church is only for Believers, **NOT** unbelievers. **Jesus did NOT tell sinners to go to church. He told His *Church* to go to sinners. We ARE His CHURCH *(Believers, Elect).***

In Rev. 2:21 *(21) And I gave her space to repent of her fornication; and she repented not.* Jesus has allowed her *(church)* this time to repent. However, using our own will that never comes to fruition.

In Rev. 2:22 *(22) Behold, I will cast her into a bed, and them that commit adultery with her into great tribulation, except they repent of their deeds.* **This is a dire warning from our Lord to those *"playing church"*.** People everywhere need to be reminded there is a ***payday*** someday. **Take God seriously.**

In Rev. 2:23 *(23) And* ***I will kill her children with death;*** *and all the churches shall know that I am he which searcheth the reins and hearts: and I will give unto every* *one of you according to your works*. This is what is ahead of all unbelievers, **Judgment Day**. Those not **In Christ** will be *Hellbound.*

In Rev. 2:24 *(24) But unto you I say, and unto the rest in Thyatira, as many as have not this doctrine, and which have not known the depths of Satan, as they speak; I will put upon you none other burden.* Certainly, Jesus is speaking first of all to those who go against Him and The Truth of His Word. He then says there is a *remnant* of His faithful and to them, He will do no harm.

In Rev. 2:25 *(25) But that which ye have already hold fast till I come.* Then, *Jesus* says He will be aware of His Elect and He tells them to hold fast, *(stay strong)* **In Him**.

In Rev. 2:26 *(26) And he that overcometh, and keepeth my works unto the end, to him will I give power over the nations:* Jesus here is saying to all those who are His; **stay strong** and keep His Works, His Commandments, and His Word. When He returns, they *(we)* will be co-rulers with Him in the **Millennial Kingdom**. This is HUGE!

In Rev. 2:27 *(27) And he shall rule them with a rod of iron; as the vessels of a potter shall they be broken to shivers: even as I received of my Father.* **Jesus will reign with a rod of iron** and His Elect will be rewarded. **This is also referring to the Millennial Kingdom to come.**

In Rev. 2:28 *(28) And I will give him the morning star.* All Believers know that Jesus is their everything, light, joy, morning star, and everlasting life.

In Rev. 2:29 *(29) He that hath an ear, let him hear what the Spirit saith unto the churches.* Jesus reiterates to all who can hear Him, such are His Sheep *(Elect)*. This is why we must evangelize. We must witness to others *(give out Bible tracts with phone# or websites)* or **give out small Gospels of John.** Saying you're a Christian and then not sharing the Gospel is an act of treason against God. Definitely, bring and *(feed)* those truly desiring God to Church or **Bible studies at your home or online! Don't be a Christian in name only!!!**

I will tell you of an incident that happened to me. I have written about this once before. I was at a local gym and I planted a seed, long story short. I gave a worker at this gym a **Gospel of John**. A few weeks went by before I saw him again, when I did his eyes lit up. He took me to the side and with tears in his eyes told me what happened. He said, "I was up that night you gave me The Gospel of John till 3 a.m." He went on to say, "And I read the Gospel of John you gave me." Then he added, **"God has opened my eyes to Jesus and I am a changed man!"** He thanked me again and again as his tears continued to roll down his face. I prayed with him, thanked Jesus, and told him it was ALL God! These are the things that go on behind the scenes. These are the things that God Orchestrates, that we know little or nothing about on this side of Heaven.

It is the highest honor and privilege to be used by God. Help those you can by spreading God's Truths, and all truths, regardless **of how many it may offend,** truth does that. We as Christians are responsible for telling others of Him and His Truths. Specifically, **being deeply hated by this world is a large part of life for each Truth-teller. Jesus has overcome the world for His Elect, rejoice!**

We love Jesus because He first Loved us. It is **not our persuasion** but His. When or **if God moves** *(quickens)* someone's heart there is a difference. It's not because we try and sell Jesus. **They must first see <u>their sins</u> as repulsive, as God sees them. This happens when Jesus *(God)* <u>initiates</u> His love into them, we don't.** Then he or she should find a Bible Teaching church that uses **Expository Preaching** *(Protestant Reformed) so* that he or she can grow in faith Biblically in all of God's Truths. This would be **a Church that teaches the doctrine of Election and the doctrine of Depravity.** A True Church makes Disciples and the beat goes on and on with the power of God.

We MUST read and study God's Word each day. It will be our food and water for spiritual growth. Amen!

Let's recap the church in Thyatira. This church allowed sin, even woman leaders! It would be described as a church of Jezebel. In America, we had a sexual revolt, then a homosexual insurgence; now, a brain-dead Gender Identity uprising. **America no longer leads in righteousness but follows in wickedness.**

I had a "Christian" friend I called the morning after the evening God Saved me. I asked him a few questions and to make a long story short, he took me to a *Benny Hinn (false convert)* event that weekend! Be careful who you ask for help! There were close to twenty years before we touched base again. I asked him if he still followed false teachers and he said no. I gave him a copy of the book *"Digging Deeper into God's Truth Defines a Christian."* We talked and I asked him "Who was that woman I saw you with?" His reply spoke volumes to me, *"Oh she has been kind to me while I was going through hard times."* I pressed on and asked, *"Are you sleeping with her?"* His reply was revealing, disheartening, and shocking, he said *"I am doing her husband a favor because he is getting old."* **Those of the world think that's funny**. I assure you God does not, nor do True Believers. It is always wise to ask personal questions. **Those In Christ will HATE sin, not laugh about it.** Those Born Again were once a servant of sin. Then through Biblical Sanctification become a faithful servant of righteousness, a Colossal Difference! Those who are false converts want autonomy before Grace. Those who are truly Born Again by God will **love what God loves and HATE what God HATES**. There are countless false converts worldwide, beware! I was one...But God... **People who aren't interested in Holy living will avoid being exposed to sound doctrine.** Indeed, **false converts are marked by bad theology and Biblical illiteracy.** They read the Bible to say what they want it to mean, rather than what it truly means. **They choose "pastors" who make them laugh**, **those who put on a show.** They will use irrelevant passages, cherry-pick verses they like, and take them out of context. Then they run you through a rabbit trail of misinterpreted scriptures to *prove* their false narratives. **God's Truths are offensive to the unbeliever and the baby Christian.**

God's Truths are taken seriously by very few; such being God's Elect. **In short, unless one builds and lives their LIFE supported by Biblical Truths, they're only deceiving themselves.** The evidence would be public and most telling. All we can do many times is plant seeds of God's Truths, pray for them, and move on…

"Religion is your seeking after a god in your own image. Christianity is God's seeking you & moving to redeem you by the death of His Son."

James Montgomery Boice, *Theologian*

"There are three types of believers, **Believers**, **Unbelievers** and **Make believers**; I was a make believer, yet I didn't even realize that at that time. This is the damage today's so-called pastors create. It's a false belief, a false jesus and false hope."

Joseph Malara, *Theologian*

Chapter 3

Commentary *Revelation Chapter 3*

In Rev. 3:1 *(1) And unto the angel of the* ***church in Sardis*** *write; These things saith he that hath the seven Spirits of God and the seven stars; I know thy works, that thou hast a name that thou livest, and art dead.* Jesus now addresses the church in Sardis. He is not at all pleased with them. Jesus says they are dead spiritually, not His. **They use His NAME but they are Spiritually Dead, and not among those who sincerely love Him, such are counterfeits.**

In Rev. 3:2 *(2) Be watchful, and strengthen the things which remain, that are ready to die: for I have not found thy works perfect before God.* This is to say that God sees all and to always be ready to work towards your eternity. **Moreover, we will EACH be judged by GOD *(Jesus)* concerning our works, good and bad.** We are never Saved by *any* "works". However, if Saved, you were NOT Saved to sit but to serve. What are YOU doing for Him today?

In Rev. 3:3 *(3) Remember therefore how thou hast received and heard, and hold fast, and repent. If therefore thou shalt not watch, I will come on thee as a thief, and thou shalt not know what hour I will come upon thee.* This is not alluding to His 2nd Coming. He tells them to repent and be ready to meet Him, *in death.* Those who are True Believers will and hope to be found serving Him.

In Rev. 3:4 *(4) Thou hast a few names even in Sardis which have not defiled their garments; and they shall walk with me in white: for they are worthy.* He says **those who live for Him** will be found in white.

In Rev. 3:5 *(5) He that overcometh, the same shall be clothed in white raiment; and I will not blot out his name out of the book of life, but I will confess his name before my Father, and before his angels.* God will never take one's name out of the Book of Life. **However, He will chastise, discipline, rebuke, and correct you as needed.** Some more than others... Many a time, before God uses a man greatly, He must first break him greatly. Falling to *rock bottom* can teach more lessons than mountain tops ever will.

In Rev. 3:6 *(6) He that hath an ear, let him hear what the Spirit saith unto the churches.* The Sheep of Jesus, His Elect hear Him and move to obey Him.

Let's recap, the *church at Sardis.* This is a dead congregation of the **lost.** Those who are among the **unredeemed, unconverted, unregenerated, aka Make-believers,** represent over 90% of today's so-called "Christian" churches. This should be a wake-up call to all who read this and study the Book of Revelation. Above all, ask yourself, is YOUR "church" or are YOU spiritually dead too? **Examine yourself against scripture and scrutinize All those who have YOUR ear, *those you listen to.*** *(See 2 Corinthians 13:5)*

In Rev. 3:7 *(7) And to the angel of the* ***church in Philadelphia*** *write; These things saith he that is holy, he that is true, he that hath the key of David, he that openeth, and no man shutteth; and shutteth, and no man* *openeth;* Jesus is proclaiming His Word is the Supreme Sovereign Authority.

In Rev. 3:8 *(8) I know thy works: behold, I have set before thee an open door, and no man can shut it: for thou hast a little strength, and hast kept my word, and hast not denied my name.* Jesus is saying that **He knows what each of us has done for or against Him.** He speaks well of His Own *(Elect)* who will never deny Him.

In Rev. 3:9 *(9) Behold, I will make them of the synagogue of Satan, which say they are Jews, and are not, but do lie; behold, I will make them to come and worship before thy feet, and to know that I have loved thee.* Hence, some were Jews in a physical sense but inside they were against God and not for Him. This is a reference to **Judgment Day when all unredeemed will kneel and profess Jesus as Lord,** *(Romans 14:11)* **then they are all thrown into Hell.** This could also reference those Christ will save during the Great Tribulation. The first 3 ½ years will be referred to as **The Tribulation**; the last 3

½ years are known as **The Great Tribulation**.

In Rev. 3:10 *(10) Because thou hast kept the word of my patience, I also will keep thee from the hour of temptation, which shall come upon all the world, to try them that dwell upon the earth.* **This is a reference to those Jesus will keep from The Tribulation; those who are eagerly waiting to be with Him. Those are His *(Elect),* True Believers; this verse concerns The *Rapture.***

In Rev. 3:11 *(11) Behold, I come quickly: hold that fast which thou hast, that no man take thy crown.* This is a warning to all Believers; **we must guard our Faith and grow in Sanctification daily to please our Lord. He will reward some personally.**

In Rev. 3:12 *(12) Him that overcometh will I make a pillar in the temple of my God, and he shall go no more out: and I will write upon him the name of my God, and the name of the city of my God, which is new Jerusalem, which cometh down out of heaven from my God: and I will write upon him my* *new name.* Jesus is saying this to His followers. He claims them and has *Marked Them* unto Himself. The Elect will be left standing when the unbelievers and false converts fall. His Redeemed will be with Him in **The New Jerusalem. This is not the Earthly Jerusalem but The Heavenly one built by God, which will come down to the New Earth.** *(more on this later)*

In Rev. 3:13 *(13) He that hath an ear, let him hear what the Spirit saith unto the churches.* **Those that belong to Jesus will heed all of His warnings and be obedient.**

Let's recap the *church in Philadelphia*. We see that Jesus speaks very well of them! He says they are His and loved by Him. **In verse 10 Jesus says He will keep them, His "Church" from the hour of temptation. This clearly says His Elect will NOT be present to experience the 7-year Tribulation but be Raptured.** There was no criticism of this Faithful Church. This city was also known as **"Brotherly Love"**. This Church was the fruit of Paul's prolonged ministry in Ephesus. This is **Biblical Christianity**, a Church True Believers must find, to grow closer to Christ in Truth each day. **It's all about Jesus Christ, not you and not me.** Remember, Jesus is always telling us to look up in anticipation, then be ready for His Return, not to look up and be ready for the "Antichrist"! **Jesus removes His Bride *(Church)* before The Tribulation.**

In Rev. 3:14 (*14) And unto the angel of the* ***church of the Laodiceans*** *write; These things saith the Amen, the faithful and true witness, the beginning of the creation of God;* This is again to say the Elder or Pastor of each church will receive this letter from God.

In Rev. 3:15 *(15) I know thy works, that thou art neither cold nor hot: I would thou wert cold or hot.* Let's unpack this very important verse. Jesus is stating the facts concerning 90% of today's so-called "Christian" churches. This was the spiritual state of the church of the Laodiceans. **This *(lukewarm condition)* is also the sad temperature of**

the whole world today towards Christ. Many people freely profess Jesus as the Christ, but show little to no evidence *(fruit)* of being His. Jesus would rather they be ice cold for Him, or on fire for Him. **Those who are lukewarm reveal nothing but being a false convert, playing a Christian.**

In Rev. 3:16 *(16) So then because thou art lukewarm, and neither cold nor hot, I will spue thee out of my mouth.* **This is what *Jesus* will do to "lukewarm Christians" send all such hypocrites to Hell.**

In Rev. 3:17 *(17) Because thou sayest, I am rich, and increased with goods, and have need of nothing; and knowest not that thou art wretched, and miserable, and poor, and blind, and naked:* This is a clear picture of reality. There are many unbelievers even professing believers who feel content with their possessions and require nothing. Moreover, **God's Elect realize they are each worthless and but dirt.** We are not deserving of His Mercy or Grace. **We know we deserve Hell. Therefore, we need Jesus**

for each breath we draw. We rely on Him for all things, each second of each day.

In Rev. 3:18 *(18) I counsel thee to buy of me gold tried in the fire, that thou mayest be rich; and white raiment, that thou mayest be clothed, and that the shame of thy nakedness do not appear; and anoint thine eyes with eyesalve, that thou mayest see.* Jesus is explaining that He alone has given us *(Elect)* so much each day, and with more to look forward to in and from Him.

In Rev. 3:19 *(19) As many* ***as I love, I rebuke and chasten:*** *be zealous therefore, and repent.* This is an image of the love *(charity)* Jesus has for His Own. He tells us to be zealous for Him and repent of our sins. **His discipline is meant to bring us to our knees and as a result, closer to Him in Truth.** He will orchestrate events in our lives that will bring us to Him in tears. This is His Love for His Elect. **I am a living witness of such love** *(Pages 280-282) Thank you, Lord.*

In Rev. 3:20 *(20) Behold, I stand at the door, and knock: if any man hear my voice,* *and open the door, I will come in to him, and will sup with him, and he with me.* **This is a rebuke to a wayward church, a church without Christ.** They may say they are believers; they may even have *Jesus's* name written on their "church" door but they are not in His Truth. **They're spiritually dead.** Overall, it's a church that is full of self-righteous, false converts. **There will be no answer to His knocking. When Jesus wants a soul, He knocks all doors down! He NEVER knocks and waits...**

In Rev. 3:21 *(21) To him that overcometh will I grant to sit with me in my throne, even as I also overcame, and am set down with my Father in his throne.* This is a figurative expression going out to each of God's Elect.

In Rev. 3:22 *(22) He that hath an ear, let him hear what the Spirit saith unto the churches.* This refers only to The Elect.

Let's recap the *church of the Laodiceans*. First of all, **Jesus is sick of this church** which resembles most "churches" today! I have personally been to many, many such **establishments,** most now labeled "non-denominational". This includes those so-called fundamental, churches of Christ, and all liberal churches. In short, Pentecostal, Charismatic, and Catholic "churches" fit into this category. This list extends to all motivational churches, those with "famous pastors" and dangerous cults with false prophets, e.g. *Ellen White, Ron Hubbard, Muhammad, all woman pastors, Joseph Smith, Charles Russell, Mary Baker Eddy,* etc. All false religious movements are filled with self-righteous, self-confident, proud, and boastful liars; those who are not Born Again by God. Their well-crafted lies give off an illusion, a cloak of Christlikeness. Moreover, their doctrine is anything but Christ-like. They are not prone to Biblical Truths and are incapable of being reasoned with. **They would rather drink the "Kool-Aid" of *Jim Jones* than accept Biblical Truths.** They are unregenerated, unconverted hypocrites with some even professing to know Christ. However, they do not belong to Him, **nor do**

they truly want to. They want only what Jesus can give e.g., health, healing, happiness, MONEY, and material things but NOT HIM or His Truths. These **false converts** possess a false emotional and spiritual enthusiasm, they appeal to gullible and undiscerning people. As a result, they have little Biblical knowledge of TRUTH. **They have no genuine desire to be corrected or to grow in Sanctification.** Then they produce more false converts *(bad fruit)* who do the same and that beat goes on and on. Then some others profess no need for a Savior, they think they're **"good enough"** or rich enough to be self-sufficient. They are caught up in the **"me" generation**. There will be large "mega-churches" that will remain on Earth, concerning The Rapture. They will be so delusional, that they will boast that the Rapture did not take place because they will still be here! Jesus found only 2 of the 7 churches good and 5 NOT good, **Hellbound.** The dead churches have no Biblical creeds, as a result, many (of their "pastors" and parishioners) **have NOT even read the whole Bible cover to cover once!**

They have no Biblical Doctrinal statement. They haven't even read such writings as the "Westminster Confession", "Baptist Confession of Faith 1689", or the "Canons of Dort". They would not embrace the clear and simple "Doctrines of Grace"! **They go against the Doctrine of Election and despise the Doctrine of Depravity.** They refuse them even after each has been explained Biblically! They won't agree with the whole Bible as the inspired, inherent, and infallible Word of God. They *(false converts)* twist God's Word and dogmatically and **actively deny God's Absolute Sovereignty**. Jesus says to them as I repeat **Revelation 3:16 LSB** *So because you are lukewarm, and neither hot nor cold, I will spit you out of My mouth.* Let's put it this way, **Jesus does NOT spit them into Heaven**. This is a valid assessment if you will, a description of 90% of today's so-called "Christian churches". However, there will be a *remnant* saved. **Those Saved, will not stay long in a false church.** Their constant need for all of God's Truths will be **openly evident.**

We as True Believers must never remain silent against false preachers, **nor should we pray for them. We must actively oppose and EXPOSE and call them out!** In Deuteronomy 18:20 ***(false prophets are put to death).*** In Titus 1:13 ***(rebuke them sharply).*** In Titus 1:11 ***(stop their mouths).*** In Titus 3:10 ***(reject them).*** In 2 John 1:9-10 ***(refuse them and not welcome them into our house).*** In Matthew 7:15 ***(they come in Sheep's clothing but are wolves).*** Matthew 24:24 ***(false signs and wonders will not fool the Elect).*** 2 Timothy 4:3-4 ***(a time will come when people will not endure sound doctrine, turning from the TRUTH).*** In Galatians 1:8 ***(Let them be ACCURSED).*** In Ephesians 5:11 ***(Expose them).*** Christians are not called to be nice, popular, or funny; **we are called to be BIBLICAL.** Let's look at **Mark 13:22** *For false Christs and false prophets shall rise and shall shew signs and wonders, to seduce, <u>if it were possible</u>, even the* ***elect.*** God's **Elect will not be fooled** by a false Jesus, false doctrines, or false miracles. **A Saved person loves to read and STUDY**

God's Word daily to find fault in himself and seek and correct doctrinal errors in others. Iron sharpens iron, and **True Believers will welcome correction. A person saved by God "Born Again" can never tolerate false teaching for long.** If the Holy Spirit has the power to save someone, create a new heart, a new creation; **He has the power to bring them OUT of false teaching!** If this is not the case with an individual, then he or she is simply a false convert and self-deceived. I know I was one for 20 years until I was Born Again by Him. **My Salvation had absolutely NOTHING to do with me, nor would anyone else's.** The only way to defend yourself against false teachings is to know God's Word like the back of your hand; **being IN CHRIST will separate Truth from Error...**

> **"God's Word is TRUTH and it will separate, Good from Evil, Light from Darkness, Justified from Guilty, Holy from Unholy, Clean from Unclean, Right from Wrong, SHEEP from Goats, and Believers from Make-believers."**
>
> Joseph Malara, *Theologian*

Chapter 4

Commentary *Revelation Chapter 4*

In Rev. 4:1 *(1) After this I looked, and, behold, a door was opened in heaven: and the first voice which I heard was as it were of a trumpet talking with me; which said, Come up hither, and I will shew thee things which must be hereafter* We see a glimpse into what God wants His Elect to better understand. When Jesus *(voice as a trumpet Rev.1:10)* says, *"Come up here, and I will show you what must take place after these things"*, what things? **After the "Church" has finished its Earthly time and is *caught up*, Raptured** *(1 Thessalonians 4:16-17).*

In Rev. 4:2-3 *(2) And immediately I was in the spirit: and, behold, a throne was set in heaven, and one sat on the throne. (3) And he that sat was to look upon like a jasper and a sardine stone: and there was a rainbow round about the throne, in sight like unto an emerald.* The Apostle is given a Heavenly vantage point, he describes in mere words what he witnesses. Notably, by chapter 4 the word “church” was used over 19 times. When you read ***four and twenty elders*** that indicates the *(Bride of Christ)* Church. The Church *(Born Again Believers; Elect)* will be Raptured before the seven years of Tribulation. In short, John was in a place, a different realm, He was **witnessing a Divine forthcoming vision of certainties.** This will all be caused by God’s Universal Sovereignty.

In Rev. 4:4 *(4) And round about the throne were four and twenty seats: and upon the seats I saw four and twenty elders sitting, clothed in white raiment; and they had on their heads crowns of gold.* There are twenty-four seats and twenty-four elders in white robes with crowns on their heads. However, all will be relinquished at the feet of Jesus. Indeed, **no one is worthy** of any Glory, fame, or salutation but Jesus. Moreover, **here we see the Church is in Heaven.** The elders represent the “The Church” from the day of Pentecost to the Rapture. These will NOT be the *Redeemed of Israel* yet, nor all of God’s Elect. These are the Saved *(The Church)* in their new Resurrected Bodies *(enhanced* *senses, incorruptible and everlasting).* We will have a body like Christ had after His Resurrection, a Glorious Body.

In Rev. 4:5 *(5) And out of the throne proceeded lightnings and thunderings and voices: and there were seven lamps of fire burning before the throne, which are the seven Spirits of God.* When God's Word uses the number seven, it means it's God's number of completion. The Apostle John witnesses God's Awesome Power.

In Rev. 4:6 *(6) And before the throne there was a sea of glass like unto crystal: and in the midst of the throne, and round about the throne, were four beasts full of eyes before and behind.* The Apostle John is describing what he is seeing.

In Rev. 4:7 *(7) And the first beast was like a lion, and the second beast like a calf, and the third beast had a face as a man, and the fourth beast was like a flying eagle.* The Apostle John uses figurative language to describe what he sees. The lion represents strength, the *(ox)* calf *carries heavy loads*, the face of a man is a *man's face*, the eagle could mean *wisdom and speed.* I have several ways to describe this verse but all are mere speculation.

In Rev. 4:8-9 *(8) And the four beasts had each of them six wings about him; and they were full of eyes within: and they rest not day and night, saying, Holy, holy, holy, Lord God Almighty, which was, and is, and is to come. (9) And when those beasts give glory and honour and thanks to him that sat on the throne, who liveth for ever and ever.* We see a type of angel, four of them expressing admiration for its maker. **There is nothing but praise on their lips to Almighty God, who was and is and is to come.**

In Rev. 4:10-11 *(10) The four and twenty elders fall down before him that sat on the throne, and worship him that liveth for ever and ever, and cast their crowns before the throne, saying, (11) Thou art worthy, O Lord, to receive glory and honour and power: for thou hast created all things, and for <u>thy pleasure,</u> they are and were created.* If you have any issues worshipping Him today; you won't like Heaven. This reveals the future life of all *(Elect)* Saints. **It will be a time of continuous nonstop worship of our Lord.**

Let's examine this 11th verse and realize for whose pleasure all things were created and exist, **His Pleasure**. This is written to those who are His Elect. This privilege has nothing to do with us and everything to do with Jesus. **Father God Chose the Bride *(Church)* for His Son Jesus. We *(Bride)* do not get to choose our Father or our Groom *(Jesus).*** Salvation and all that is pleasing to God, comes from Him. Let's remember it was **the Creator who set out to *redeem* His creation, not the other way around**. We are nothing but dirt and He is Everything! The Shepherd seeks after His Sheep. **The Sheep never go looking for their Shepherd.**

Jesus: "It is Written."

Satan: "Is it Written?"

KNOW THE DIFFERENCE

Chapter 5

Commentary *Revelation Chapter 5*

In Rev. 5:1 *(1) And I saw in the right hand of him that sat on the throne a book written within and on the backside, sealed with seven seals.* There is a Book *(scroll)* in Heaven that has seven seals and no one in all of Heaven is worthy to open it, but Jesus. He is the Sacrificial Lamb who bled and died on behalf of sinners, this makes Him Worthy. It is the Deed to the World, even the universe. Let's visit **Psalm 2:8 LSB** *Ask of Me, and I will surely give the nations as Your inheritance, And the ends of the earth as Your possession.* The Father gives it all to the Son.

Meanwhile, those on Earth are going through *(God's Wrath)* **The Apocalypse**. It started in chapter 4 and continues until The 2nd Coming. **When that time comes all prophecies will be fulfilled.**

In Rev. 5:2 *(2) And I saw a strong angel proclaiming with a loud voice, Who is worthy to open the book, and to loose the seals* *thereof?* This angel in Heaven is asking, "Is anyone worthy to open the seals?"

In Rev. 5:3 *(3) And no man in heaven, nor in earth, neither under the earth, was able to open the book, neither to look thereon.* **There will be no one able, nor would any dare try to even look upon it.**

In Rev. 5:4 *(4) And I wept much, because no man was found worthy to open and to read the book, neither to look thereon.* The Apostle John came to tears.

In Rev. 5:5 *(5) And one of the elders saith unto me, Weep not: behold, the* ***Lion*** *of the tribe of Judah, the Root of David, hath prevailed to open the book, and to loose the seven seals thereof.* There is only **One** who can open the Seals. **He is the Son of Man, Lord of Lords Himself, Jesus, The Christ.**

In Rev. 5:6 *(6) And I beheld, and, lo, in the midst of the throne and of the four beasts, and in the midst of the elders,* ***stood a Lamb as it had been slain,*** *having seven horns and seven eyes, which are the seven Spirits* *of God sent forth into all the earth.* The Lamb who was slain is Jesus. The number seven signifies complete and perfect Divine Power.

In Rev. 5:7 *(7) And he came and took the book out of the right hand of him that sat upon the throne.* **Jesus will go to the Throne of His Father** and He will take the Book *(scroll)* out of His Father's Right Hand.

In Rev. 5:8 *(8) And when he had taken the book, the four beasts and four and twenty elders fell down before the Lamb, having every one of them harps, and golden vials full of odours, which are the prayers of saints.* This will be a spectacular sight when God's Elect who were Raptured and those who died before that day In Christ, will one day witness this event. Furthermore, until Jesus comes or calls us Home, **we live only in the power of God.**

In Rev. 5:9 *(9) "And they sung a new song, saying, Thou art worthy to take the book, and to open the seals thereof: for thou wast slain, and hast redeemed us to God by thy blood out of every kindred, and tongue,* *and people, and nation;"* There will be a New Song we will sing in Heaven. It will praise Jesus the Redeemer of His Saints. We will be in our Resurrected Bodies singing to our Lord Jesus. There is nothing that could come close, in our wildest imaginations that will mirror such a marvelous and joyful time!

In Rev. 5:10 *(10) And hast made us unto our God kings and priests: and we shall reign on the earth.* This is to say those In Christ are considered ministers of His Word. This verse refers to The **Millennial Kingdom**, where we *(Elect)* will reign alongside Jesus for a thousand years.

In Rev. 5:11 *(11) And I beheld, and I heard the voice of many angels round about the throne and the beasts and the elders: and the number of them was ten thousand times ten thousand, and thousands of thousands;* The Apostle John is describing an awesome sight to behold and too many to count.

In Rev. 5:12 *(12) Saying with a loud voice, Worthy is the Lamb that was slain to receive power, and riches, and wisdom, and* *strength, and honour, and glory, and blessing.* **All of Heaven will praise the Lord of Lords for Who He Is, and for what He has done and what He will do.**

In Rev. 5:13-14 *(13) And every creature which is in heaven, and on the earth, and under the earth, and such as are in the sea, and all that are in them, heard I saying, Blessing, and honour, and glory, and power, be unto him that sitteth upon the throne, and unto the Lamb for ever and ever. (14) And the four beasts said, Amen. And the four and twenty elders fell down and worshipped him that liveth for ever and ever.* The entire universe will hear these Heavenly Praises.

Meanwhile, down on Earth, there is total mayhem. In Heaven there is no time, space, or matter as we know it here. On the other hand, **try and imagine the uproar, the chaos of the first day of the Rapture, and what that will bring.** There will be airplane crashes, train, bus, and car crashes, and medical emergencies, everywhere worldwide; a disarray of mass confusion, and occasions for more and more crime. This will all happen within moments of Jesus taking up *(Rapture)* His *(Church, Bride, Born Again Believers).* When all of God's Elect on Earth are gone, all Christians are gone and The Holy Spirit *(Comforter, Holy Ghost, Restrainer)* will also be gone. He resides in the hearts of Born Again by God Believers. The balance of those left behind would all be Godless and bankrupt of morals. People will just be interested in themselves, also **left behind will be hundreds of millions of *false converts.***

Let's turn to **Matthew 23:28 LSB** *In this way, you also outwardly appear righteous to men, but inwardly you are full of hypocrisy and lawlessness.* This is Jesus speaking to those who truly thought they were righteous, the *Scribes* and *Pharisees* the most religious of their day. He *(Jesus)* goes on to call them **hypocrites**. There will be **countless religious people left behind**. I remember when a relative of mine read my 5th book "Digging Deeper into God's Truth Defines a Christian". He remarked afterward saying, “It seems hard for man to get to Heaven”. The point is that it is impossible for man; only possible with God. Above all, as a result of The Rapture, the full exposure of human depravity will be set loose. Therefore, man’s full desire to sin more and more will run rampant. Let’s turn to **1 John 2:16** ***For all that is in the world, the lust of the flesh, and the lust of the eyes, and the pride of life, is not of the Father, but is of the world.*** It will be a dark time, a time of great destruction, where evil has a field day. The people will be **proud and boastful of their sins**, finding their comfort in **wicked sexual perversions.** This chaos will make the Godless democratic insane riots of BLM, & George Floyd debacles look tame. That useless uncontrollable mob violence lasted months and many were killed by the racist and evil surge of their own “Peaceful Demonstrations”. That devastation was all executed under the guise of “social justice”. This Divine moment *(Rapture)* will be many times worse on Earth. **This chaos will occur simultaneously in all nations worldwide!**

There will be little to no restraint against muggings, thugs, robberies, lootings, riots, and gangs. **Love and morality would be nonexistent. It would be like a liberal agenda paradise, a utopia for the criminal-minded,** e.g., theft, rape, assaults, mayhem, and murder. This will be an opportunity for the progressives *(Leftists)* to destroy more of the world through fires and pure EVIL. **This would all happen on DAY ONE, of the Rapture!**

It will only get worse and worse. When people realize so many are gone, **they will think of UFOs, Aliens, Spacemen, and all types of nonsense.** They will not think of Biblical Christianity or The God of The Bible. They will not believe in Jesus, His Gospel, His Wrath, or His Plan. They will find alternative reasons why so many disappeared. Then some will even believe that their "god" has taken away the wicked!

There will be countless false teachers and false preachers popping up. However, some may realize after a while what happened, that their riches, fame, and false doctrine further exposed their phoniness, lies, greed, and deceit. **Their belief was not in God for Jesus but in themselves for recognition, pride, notoriety, and money.** They're deceived deceivers having a reprobate mind out to deceive others. **This is why I write, to get many away from their enticing false teachers, escalated misguided influences, and twisted false beliefs.**

Let's turn to **Matthew 7:21-23 NASB** *(21) "Not everyone who says to Me, 'Lord, Lord,' will enter the kingdom of heaven, but the one who does the will of My Father who is in heaven will enter. (22) Many will say to Me on that day, 'Lord, Lord, did we not prophesy in Your name, and in Your name cast out demons, and in Your name perform many miracles?' (23) And then I will declare to them, "I never knew you; leave Me, you who practice lawlessness."* Above all, take notice of **those Jesus is talking about** here. They say they know Him, **they call Him Lord, Lord**, then go on to say that by using **His Name** *(Jesus)* they cast out demons, prophesied, and performed many miracles. **This is a huge sign regarding the false Charismatic, Apostolic, and Pentecostal movements.** Those and many others today falsely use the name of Jesus. However, unbeknownst to them they are tapping into the powers of Satan. They all profess to know Jesus. In contrast, **Jesus says, "I Never Knew You..." These are the four most feared words in the Bible!** There is yet one verse that all false converts cling to, **John 3:16**; that verse is a **declaration by God** toward His Believing Elect and **not an invitation** for Salvation. Let's turn to **John 17:9 ESV** *I (Jesus) am praying for them (Elect). I am* ***not*** *praying for the world (unredeemed) but for those whom you (Father) have given me, for they are yours.* **Either you're all Christ's in all His Truths, or not His because of yours.** God's Truths are unveiled through all of scripture. Certainly, in The Book of Revelation.

> **"There is nothing here on Earth that is worth a man's pursuit except God."**
>
> Charles Spurgeon, *The Prince of Pastors*

Chapter 6

Commentary *Revelation Chapter 6*

In Rev. 6:1-2 *(1) "**And I saw when the Lamb opened one of the seals**, and I heard, as it were the noise of thunder, one of the four beasts saying, Come and see." (2) "And I saw, and behold a white horse: and he that sat on him had a bow; and a crown was given unto him: and he went forth conquering, and to conquer."* Jesus opens the ***First Seal***. There will come a very deceitful man who arises on the scene. The **white horse** symbolizes a **false peace**. He will be a **type of Caesar** and to the **Muslims their Mahdi**. **He will promise world peace, unity, and love.**

The whole world will designate him as their king. They will embrace him as their only hope, their god-type of leader. The whole world will believe in his big lie of world peace. He will be the **Antichrist**. There will continue to be false messiahs popping up as there are today, but more so.

The **Antichrist** will usher in a "One World Government", as a "One World Leader", a "One World Religion" using a "One World Currency". This of course **Happens AFTER The Church is Raptured.** There are many today not looking up, not preparing for Jesus's Return. They are incorrectly looking inward for the Antichrist today. **He will not come until all Believers go up!**

In Rev. 6:3-4 the short-lived peace is over. *(3) And when he had opened the second seal, I heard the second beast say, Come and see. (4) And there went out another horse that was red: and power was given to him that sat thereon to take peace from the earth, and that they should kill one another: and there was given unto him a great sword.* Jesus opens the ***Second Seal.*** The **red horse** signifies worldwide **WAR**. **There will be countless violent slaughters and great human loss. There will be people killing others for no reason at all!** Truly, just pure unrestrained evil on full display, **human depravity**.

In Rev. 6:5-6 *(5) And when he had opened the third seal, I heard the third beast say, Come and see. And I beheld, and lo a black horse; and he that sat on him had a pair of balances in his hand. (6) "And I heard a voice in the midst of the four beasts say, A measure of wheat for a penny, and three measures of barley for a penny; and see thou hurt not the oil and the wine."* Jesus opens the ***Third Seal*** in Heaven. The **black horse** represents **famine**. There will be global hunger like never before. There will be food lines, shortages, rationing and **many will die of starvation. *Fake News* will claim it's all due to *climate change!* The cost of all food will skyrocket. People will kill for it.**

In Rev. 6:7-8 LSB *(7) And when He opened the fourth seal, I heard the voice of the fourth living creature saying, "Come." (8) Then I looked, and behold, a pale horse; and he who sits on it had the name Death, and* ***Hades*** *was following with him. Authority was given to them over a fourth of the earth, to kill with sword and with famine and with pestilence and by the wild beasts of the earth.*

Jesus opens the ***Fourth Seal***. The **pale horse** represents **Death**. God allows for the first time in all of history, the death of a quarter of the population of the world; **that will be over two billion people who will die**. **In short, *Hades* is a temporary holding place where the unredeemed dead will wait for the Final Judgment.** There will be mass burials implemented; **each day will be worse than the day before.**

What most people don't understand is that **God is Sovereign**. **God has the full right to destroy me or take my life, your life, or allow it to be taken.** Indeed, our **sin** is so appalling and nauseating before Him. This means God can take anyone's life at any given moment. This is with no excuse or explanation and with no questions asked, **solely for His Pleasure and His Purpose**. He is God, and we are not. **Proverbs 16:4** *The Lord hath made all things for himself: yea, even the wicked for the day of evil.*

In Rev. 6:9-10 *(9) And when he had opened the fifth seal, I saw under the altar the* *souls of them that were slain for the word of God, and for the testimony which they held: (10) And they cried with a loud voice, saying, How long, O Lord, holy and true, dost thou not judge and avenge our blood on them that dwell on the earth?* Jesus opens the ***Fifth Seal*** in Heaven. This seal represents all of the collective prayers **of the Saints for vengeance**. These Christians were martyred for the Word of God. **Also, notice the Redeemed Saints *(Elect)*, they're not crying out nor praying for the salvation of those who murdered them. They cry out for revenge and God's Judgment on them.** There is always a point of no return, a point when enough is enough and you want Justice. This will be midway through the 7-year Tribulation.

In Rev. 6:11-12 *(11) And white robes were given unto every one of them; and it was said unto them, that they should rest yet for a little season, until their fellowservants also and their brethren, that should be killed as they were, should be fulfilled. (12) And I beheld when he had opened the sixth seal,* *and, lo, there was a great earthquake; and the sun became black as sackcloth of hair, and the moon became as blood;* Therefore, God in His Perfect Time will answer the prayers of those martyred; He will then let loose His Vengeance. Jesus opens the ***Sixth Seal***. God will unleash **great earthquakes** worldwide. The heat and ash from this will cause a blackening in the sky, blocking the sun and causing a reddish color. These Divine catastrophic earthly disturbances will include volcanic eruptions worldwide. **This will be real Divine *Climate Change!***

In Rev. 6:13-14 *(13) And the stars of heaven fell unto the earth, even as a fig tree casteth her untimely figs, when she is shaken of a mighty wind. (14) And the heaven departed as a scroll when it is rolled together; and every mountain and island were moved out of their places.* The **Olivet Discourse** also mentions the falling of the stars in **Matthew 24:29** *Immediately after the tribulation of those days shall the sun be darkened, and the moon shall not give her light, and the stars shall fall from heaven, and the powers of the* *heavens shall be shaken:* There will be great Divine world turbulences, and supernatural phenomena will ensue.

This is also seen in **Isaiah 34:4 LSB** *And all the host of heaven will rot away, And the sky will be rolled up like a scroll; All their hosts will also wither away As a leaf withers from the vine, Or as one withers from the fig tree.* Heaven will feel this Divine firestorm, huge asteroids, meteor showers including gigantic earthquakes, which will greatly alter the core foundation of the Earth.

In Rev. 6:15-16 *(15) And the kings of the earth, and the great men, and the rich men, and the chief captains, and the mighty men, and every bondman, and every free man, hid themselves in the dens and in the rocks of the mountains; (16) And said to the mountains and rocks, Fall on us, and hide us from the face of him that sitteth on the throne, and from the wrath of the Lamb:* People flee to hide and escape but there is nowhere to hide; this is called "The Great Day of the Lamb". This is a paradox; it is more like the great day of God's Wrath. The Wrath of Jesus *(Lamb)* will accomplish all He says it will.

In Rev. 6:17 *(17) For the great day of his wrath is come; and who shall be able to stand?* Frankly, **who shall be able to stand?** This prophecy was also revealed in **Joel 2:11** *And the Lord shall utter his voice before his army: for his camp is very great: for he is strong that executeth his word: for the day of the Lord is great and very terrible; and who can abide it?* No one! In God's Divine Providence, all that He wants to die, will. Certainly, each person's timely demise was predetermined by God in His infinite Wisdom from Eternity Past. There are never any mishaps or accidents concerning God. **There is no such thing as chance or luck; only God's Favor, Mercy, Grace, or Wrath.**

> **"All things are Ordained by God and settled by Him, according to His Wise and Holy Predestination. Whatever happens here happens not by chance, but according to the Counsel of The Most High."**
>
> Charles H. Spurgeon, *The Prince of Pastors*

Chapter 7

Commentary *Revelation Chapter 7*

In Rev. 7:1-2 *(1) And after these things I saw four angels standing on the four corners of the earth, holding the four winds of the earth, that the wind should not blow on the earth, nor on the sea, nor on any tree. (2) And I saw another angel ascending from the east, having the <u>seal of the living God</u>: and he cried with a loud voice to the four angels, to whom it was given to hurt the earth and the sea,* The words "after these things" talks about the proceeding judgments up to this future moment. The four winds refer to the North, South, East and West. The *seal* in this instance means a mark of ownership, this being the **Mark of God**.

In Rev. 7:3-4 *(3) Saying, Hurt not the earth, neither the sea, nor the trees, till we have sealed the servants of our God in their foreheads. (4) And I heard the number of them which were sealed: and there were sealed an hundred and forty and four thousand of all the tribes of the children of Israel.* The

144,000 are Redeemed Jews taken from the 12 Tribes of the Sons of Israel. Twelve thousand **men** will be taken from each of the 12 Tribes; **they will receive a Mark as the Servants of God granting their protection.**

Let's look at **Jeremiah 31:33** *But this shall be the covenant that I will (God) make with the house of Israel; After those days, saith the Lord, I will put my law in their inward parts, and write it in their hearts; and will be their God, and they shall be my people.* **We can see that GOD is in full control of all things, this includes of course His Promise to Israel. Above all, His Process of Election stands firm throughout history, past, present, and future.**

In Rev. 7:5-8 *(5) Of the tribe of **Juda** were sealed twelve thousand. Of the tribe of **Reuben** were sealed twelve thousand. Of the tribe of **Gad** were sealed twelve thousand. (6) Of the tribe of **Aser** were sealed twelve thousand. Of the tribe of **Nephthalim** were sealed twelve thousand. Of the tribe of **Manasses** were sealed twelve thousand. (7)*

Of the tribe of ***Simeon*** *were sealed twelve thousand. Of the tribe of* ***Levi*** *were sealed twelve thousand. Of the tribe of* ***Issachar*** *were sealed twelve thousand. (8) Of the tribe of* ***Zabulon*** *were sealed twelve thousand. Of the tribe of* ***Joseph*** *were sealed twelve thousand. Of the tribe of* ***Benjamin*** *were sealed twelve thousand.* These verses reveal the 12 Tribes by name. There will be **12,000 men** from each tribe of Israel; totaling **144,000 Redeemed Jews.** They are chosen by God, from the tribe of Juda, Reuben, Gad, Aser, Nepthalim, Manasses, Simeon, Levi, Issachar, Zabulon, Joseph, and Benjamin.

In Rev. 7:9-10 *(9) After this I beheld, and, lo, a great multitude, which no man could number, of all nations, and kindreds, and people, and tongues, stood before the throne, and before the Lamb, clothed with white robes, and palms in their hands; (10) And cried with a loud voice, saying, Salvation to our God which sitteth upon the throne, and unto the Lamb.* There will be a great multitude of all God's Redeemed, they will be of all races and nations clothed in white robes. **They will all be crying out that Salvation belongs to God, recognizing Jesus is Salvation. Amen!**

In Rev. 7:11 *(11) And all the angels stood round about the throne, and about the elders and the four beasts, and fell before the throne on their faces, and worshipped God.* We see total non-stop conformity *(Oneness)* concerning worship in Heaven.

In Rev. 7:12 *(12) Saying, Amen: Blessing, and glory, and wisdom, and thanksgiving, and honour, and power, and might, be unto our God for ever and ever. Amen.* There will be nothing but nonstop love and praise for God and *The Lamb*, Jesus.

In Rev. 7:13 *(13) And one of the elders answered, saying unto me, What are these which are arrayed in white robes? and whence came they?* The white robes speak of purity and holiness, In Christ.

In Rev. 7:14 *(14) And I said unto him, Sir, thou knowest. And he said to me, These are they which came out of great tribulation,* *and have washed their robes, and made them white in the blood of the Lamb.* The ones whom The Apostle John asks about are the ***Tribulation Saints***. They were **not** Raptured with the Church. They will become Redeemed *(Saved)* during The Tribulation. Those who will go through all or part of The Tribulation will be recognized in Heaven. Let's look at **Matthew 24:14 LSB** *And this gospel of the kingdom shall be proclaimed in the whole world as a witness to all the nations, and <u>then the end will come</u>.*

In Rev. 7:15 *(15) Therefore are they before the throne of God, and serve him day and night in his temple: and he that sitteth on the throne shall dwell among them.* We see true recognition and uninterrupted worship of our Lord and Savior.

In Rev. 7:16-17 *(16) They shall hunger no more, neither thirst any more; neither shall the sun light on them, nor any heat. (17) For the Lamb which is in the midst of the throne shall feed them, and shall lead them unto living fountains of waters: and God shall wipe* *away all tears from their eyes.* These are the ones who will be Saved **during the 7 years of Tribulation**. The 144,000 witnesses will triumphantly **preach** and spread the gospel to those remaining on Earth. **In doing so, countless people will come to the Lord**. The Lord says He will wipe their tears away. **The Prophets and Apostles of the Bible were NOT celebrities.** They were outcasts, criminals, unpopular, and **sought after to be killed. Today, we deserve no better.**

"No Doctrine in the whole Word of God has more excited the hatred of mankind than the Truth of Absolute Sovereignty of GOD."

Charles H. Spurgeon, *"The Prince of Pastors"*

"A dog barks when his master is attacked. I would be a coward if I saw that God's Truth is attacked and yet would remain silent."

John Calvin, *Pastor-Theologian*

Chapter 8

Commentary *Revelation Chapter 8*

In Rev. 8:1-2 *(1) And when he had opened the seventh seal, there was silence in heaven about the space of half an hour. (2) And I saw the seven angels which stood before God, and to them were given seven trumpets.* Jesus opens the ***Seventh Seal***. There will be **a calm before the storm,** indicating anticipation. Then there will be seven angels with trumpets standing before God. They will announce **more of the outpouring of Wrath, these will all be God's Righteous Judgments.**

In Rev. 8:3-5 *(3) And another angel came and stood at the altar, having a golden censer; and there was given unto him much incense, that he should offer it with the prayers of all saints upon the golden altar which was before the throne. (4) And the smoke of the incense, which came with the prayers of the saints, ascended up before God out of the angel's hand. (5) And the angel took the censer, and filled it with fire of the altar,* *and cast it into the earth: and there were voices, and thunderings, and lightnings, and an earthquake.* These verses speak of the **prayers of the Saints for judgment** on their oppressors, mixed with incense before the Throne of God. **God hears and answers the prayers of His Elect, in His Time.** There will be more and more thunder, lightning, voices and earthquakes displaying God's overwhelming Wrath upon the Earth.

In Rev. 8:6-7 *(6) And the seven angels which had the seven trumpets prepared themselves to sound. (7) The first angel sounded, and there followed hail and fire mingled with blood, and they were cast upon the earth: and the third part of trees was burnt up, and all green grass was burnt up.* The ***First Trumpet*** sounds. There are no more Seals to open. This **signifies the start of the 2nd half of The Tribulation aka "The Great Tribulation".** There will be more Divine Wrath centered upon rebellious men. There will be **hail and fire** and more intensity of Earthly damage. A third of all the trees worldwide will be burned up as well as vegetation. The waters will appear red from the lava and pollutants, or turn to blood. There is a resemblance between the Plagues in Egypt *(Exodus 7-13)* and the *Trumpet Judgments* as literal judgments.

In Rev. 8:8-9 *(8) And the second angel sounded, and as it were a great mountain burning with fire was cast into the sea: and the third part of the sea became blood; (9) And the third part of the creatures which were in the sea, and had life, died; and the third part of the ships were destroyed.* The ***Second Trumpet*** sounds. Then one-third of the sea, which occupies the largest part of the Earth's surface will **become as blood**. They will possibly be hit by a large meteor; this will abolish one-third of all the ships. **This will also cause one-third of all the fish and marine life to be destroyed, worldwide.**

In Rev. 8:10-11 *(10) And the third angel sounded, and there fell a great star from heaven, burning as it were a lamp, and it fell upon the third part of the rivers, and upon the fountains of waters; (11) And the* *name of the star is called Wormwood: and the third part of the waters became wormwood; and many men died of the waters, because they were made bitter.* The ***Third Trumpet*** sounds. The Earth's **water supply will be reduced greatly**. The water that remains will cause sickness and death. This will be caused by many great-sized comets, smashing into rivers, reservoirs, and springs, worldwide.

In Rev. 8:12-13 *(12) And the fourth angel sounded, and the third part of the sun was smitten, and the third part of the moon, and the third part of the stars; so as the third part of them was darkened, and the day shone not for a third part of it, and the night likewise. (13) And I beheld, and heard an angel flying through the midst of heaven, saying with a loud voice, Woe, woe, woe, to the inhabiters of the earth by reason of the other voices of the trumpet of the three angels, which are yet to sound!* The ***Fourth Trumpet*** sounds and more catastrophic damage will take place on Earth. God will **reduce the sunlight. Therefore, severe cold will be**

upon all the Earth with darkness. These first four trumpets were inconceivable. However, the next three will be even worse!

An angel will fly over the Earth with a loud voice declaring **woe**, **woe**, **woe** signifying the worst is yet to come…

"A man does NOT become a Christian by making a decision. He is made a Christian by God, who had marked him out before the foundation of the world and sees to it that he is Born Again and that he believes in HIM."

Martyn Lloyd Jones, *Pastor*

"I am NOT permitted to let my love be so merciful as to TOLERATE and Endure False Doctrine."

Martin Luther, *Theologian - Reformer*

"Paul and Silas in *Acts 16* were in jail and still worshipped God. It's not about you or your circumstances, but Who God Is."

Joseph Malara, *Theologian*

Chapter 9

Commentary Revelation Chapter 9

In Rev. 9:1-2 *(1) And the fifth angel sounded, and I saw a star fall from heaven unto the earth: and to him was given the key of the bottomless pit. (2) And he opened the bottomless pit; and there arose a smoke out of the pit, as the smoke of a great furnace; and the sun and the air were darkened by reason of the smoke of the pit.* The ***Fifth Trumpet*** sounds. This will represent another wicked angel *(demon)*, he will be released from Heaven to go down to the abyss *(bottomless pit)*. He will release a swarm of **demonized creatures** filling the Earth as locusts. The countless amount of newly released demons causes darkness. **They will be released and seen as smoke further blackening the air.**

Let's turn to ***Jude 1: 6-7*** *And the angels which kept not their first estate, but left their own habitation, he hath reserved in everlasting chains under darkness unto the judgment of the great day. Even as Sodom and Gomorrha, and the cities about them in* *like manner, giving themselves over to fornication, and going after strange flesh, are set forth for an example, suffering the vengeance of eternal fire.* These are fallen angels *(demons)* who went against God. Their apostasy started in *(Genesis 6:2),* they went after and into women sexually. Therefore, God delivered them into chains *(Tartarus, Bottomless Pit)* until Final Judgment. They too will be released at this future time to cause more demonic devastation on Earth.

In Rev. 9:3-4 *(3) And there came out of the smoke locusts upon the earth: and unto them was given power, as the scorpions of the earth have power. (4) And it was commanded them that they should not hurt the grass of the earth, neither any green thing, neither any tree; but only those men which have not the seal of God in their foreheads.* This speaks of locusts out to destroy. However, these will not be regular locusts or regular scorpions. These are a form of demons similar to locusts that will bring a swarming desolation to whoever is in their path. They will be instructed by God not to harm the vegetation. Their instructions are to **hurt only** those people who do **NOT** have the **Seal of God** *(Mark of God)* on their foreheads.

In Rev. 9:5-6 *(5) And to them it was given that they should not kill them, but that they should be tormented five months: and their torment was as the torment of a scorpion, when he striketh a man. (6) And in those days shall men seek death, and shall not find it; and shall desire to die, and death shall flee from them.* God will use evil spirits for His Glory, in the destruction of rebellious humanity. The normal life cycle of a locust is five months. Those bitten and harmed by these unnatural creatures, *locusts* and *scorpions* will not die, nor could they. **God will keep them alive for more torture during this time. People will suffer in unspeakable severe relentless agony.**

In Rev. 9:7-12 *(7) And the shapes of the locusts were like unto horses prepared unto battle; and on their heads were as it were crowns like gold, and their faces were as the faces of men. (8) And they had hair as the hair* *of women, and their teeth were as the teeth of lions. (9) And they had breastplates, as it were breastplates of iron; and the sound of their wings was as the sound of chariots of many horses running to battle. (10) And they had tails like unto scorpions, and there were stings in their tails: and their power was to hurt men five months. (11) And they had a king over them, which is the angel of the bottomless pit, whose name in the Hebrew tongue is Abaddon, but in the Greek tongue hath his name Apollyon. (12) One woe is past; and, behold, there come two woes more hereafter.* We can see here in verses 7-12 that the creatures who are being described are like nothing we have ever seen. They will be **indestructible & evil**. Their destruction will continue for five months, worldwide.

There is a "king" over them named "Abaddon". In Hebrew and in Greek "Apollyon" means "Destroyer". He is most likely a **high-ranking demon** *(fallen angel)* in Satan's army. This is only the ***first "woe"*** there are two more to go.

In Rev. 9:13-16 *(13) And the sixth angel sounded, and I heard a voice from the four horns of the golden altar which is before God, (14) Saying to the sixth angel which had the trumpet, Loose the four angels which are bound in the great river Euphrates. (15) And the four angels were loosed, which were prepared for an hour, and a day, and a month, and a year, for to slay the third part of men. (16) And the number of the army of the horsemen were two hundred thousand thousand: and I heard the number of them.* The ***Sixth Trumpet*** is sounded. The sound of this releases four fallen angels *(demons)*. God uses more of the demonic forces to do His Bidding. This **demon army** will be **two hundred million strong**! They will be commanded to **put to death, one-third of all the remaining people on Earth**. If Jesus came this year this number translates to approximately two to four billion people.

The demons impersonate the countless idols the world creates. People worship such idols and false doctrines, including a false *jesus,* in place of the Living God and His

Written Word. Certainly, demons can take many forms to frighten and cause permanent damage and carnage. However, those alive then would rather take drugs to dull the pain and turn to their false idols. People will remain in disobedience and rebellion against the Jesus of the Bible. Their hearts harden more against God and so will their sinful ways. They will not repent, nor want to.

This will be the worst time on Earth, worse than the days of Sodom and Gomorrah; at that time God inflicted a urious quicker *first death.* There His Wrath was deadly fast upon the wicked homosexuals and their evil perversions. In his future time, God will supply those living with a slow and painful torment. Yet, by this ime billions of people have already died and billions more will soon meet the same fate, worldwide.

In Rev. 9:17-18 *(17) And thus I saw the horses in the vision, and them that sat on hem, having breastplates of fire, and of acinth, and brimstone: and the heads of the* *horses were as the heads of lions; and out of their mouths issued fire and smoke and brimstone. (18) By these three was the third part of men killed, by the fire, and by the smoke, and by the brimstone, which issued out of their mouths.* The Apostle John is referring to **only 3** demonic creatures. They will be used as God's Executioners. **Their powers will kill one-third of all mankind at this future point in time.** Many ignorant "Christian" denominations believe they can bind Satan and his demons. This is only a part of the endless false teachings of Charismatics and Pentecostals.

In Rev. 9:19 *(19) For their power is in their mouth, and in their tails: for their tails were like unto serpents, and had heads, and with them they do hurt.* The Apostle John continues to describe the terror, death, and destruction. **He is witnessing this future time as if it were happening that day.**

In Rev. 9:20 *(20) And the rest of the men which were not killed by these plagues yet repented not of the works of their hands,* *that they should not worship devils, and idols of gold, and silver, and brass, and stone, and of wood: which neither can see, nor hear, nor walk:* We see a full presentation of man's inner **depravity** on display. As a result, many bow down to the creation, rather than The Creator. This verse reminds me of the false Catholic religion. Many will be seen worshiping, holding, clinging and even praying to an inanimate object. They use rosary beads, sculptures, pictures, crosses with a false jesus, or statues of Mary! They will also use other idol figurines and even images *(pictures)* of a man-made *jesus* as their *god.* All are Abominations to God.

In Rev. 9:21 *(21) Neither repented they of their murders, nor of their sorceries, nor of their fornication, nor of their thefts.* There is only One Savior; Jesus The Christ. **We must worship Him in Spirit and TRUTH.** There will be none even then wanting to worship and cry out to the God of the Bible. Their true idols are **self, money, drugs, sex, success, control, power,** and other false *(beliefs)* gods...

Chapter 10

Commentary *Revelation Chapter 10*

In Rev. 10:1 *(1) And I saw another mighty angel come down from heaven, clothed with a cloud: and a rainbow was upon his head, and his face was as it were the sun, and his feet as pillars of fire:* This will be a high-ranking angel. **The rainbow is a reminder of what God would never do again, flood the Earth.**

In Rev. 10:2 *(2) And he had in his hand a little book open: and he set his right foot upon the sea, and his left foot on the earth.* This **little book** is a *(Deed)* claiming the sea and the Earth.

In Rev. 10:3 *(3) And cried with a loud voice, as when a lion roareth: and when he had cried, seven thunders uttered their voices.* This is a warning of what is coming.

In Rev. 10:4 *(4) And when the seven thunders had uttered their voices, I was about to write: and I heard a voice from heaven saying unto me, Seal up those things which* *the seven thunders uttered, and write them not.* It was not yet time to move forward and John was told not to write what he just heard, yet.

In Rev. 10:5-6 *(5) And the angel which I saw stand upon the sea and upon the earth lifted up his hand to heaven, (6) And sware by him that liveth for ever and ever, who created heaven, and the things that therein are, and the earth, and the things that therein are, and the sea, and the things which are therein, that there should be time no longer:* The angel will take an oath to God in Heaven and then move to do God's Bidding.

In Rev. 10:7 *(7) But in the days of the voice of the seventh angel, when he shall begin to sound, the mystery of God should be finished, as he hath declared to his servants the prophets.* This is an acknowledgment that God is ready to reveal what He promised to the Prophets of old. **God will punish all sinners not covered by His Son's death, then usher in the Kingdom of His Son.**

In Rev. 10:8 *(8) And the voice which I heard from heaven spake unto me again, and said, Go and take the little book which is open in the hand of the angel which standeth upon the sea and upon the earth.* The Apostle John is told by God to go take that **little book** from the angel.

In Rev. 10:9-10 *(9) And I went unto the angel, and said unto him, Give me the little book. And he said unto me, Take it, and eat it up; and it shall make thy belly bitter, but it shall be in thy mouth sweet as honey. (10) And I took the little book out of the angel's hand, and ate it up; and it was in my mouth sweet as honey: and as soon as I had eaten it, my belly was bitter.* This is saying, how very sweet God's Mercy and Grace are. Subsequently, for the Believer reading of such love is overwhelming and **completely unmerited.** The Believer knows he or she had nothing to do with their salvation because it was gifted to them by God alone. **The bitterness comes when we realize, that the many unconverted souls we know and love will not experience God's Grace.**

In contrast, they will experience God's Wrath and His Divine Retribution.

In Rev. 10:11 *(11) And he said unto me, Thou must prophesy again before many peoples, and nations, and tongues, and kings.* The Apostle John is to make certain this letter *(Book of Revelation)* gets out to the 7 churches. Then, the Apostle John must teach and preach these Truths far and wide. This too has been accomplished.

"Men treat God's Sovereignty as a theme for controversy, but in Scripture, it is a matter for Worship."

J. I. Packer, *Theologian*

"If Jesus Christ isn't enough to motivate you to live Biblically, you don't know Him at all."

Paul Washer, *Pastor - Evangelist*

"There is an immense DIFFERENCE BETWEEN believing in Christ and Being IN CHRIST."

Joseph Malara, *Theologian*

Chapter 11

Commentary *Revelation Chapter 11*

In Rev. 11:1-2 *(1) And there was given me a reed like unto a rod: and the angel stood, saying, Rise, and measure the temple of God, and the altar, and them that worship therein. (2) But the court which is without the temple leave out, and measure it not; for it is given unto the Gentiles: and the holy city shall they tread under foot forty and two months.* The Apostle John is given the task of measuring. The beginnings of measurements in the Old or New Testament indicate that God is dealing with the Nation of Israel.

The forty-two months represent the end of the first half of The Tribulation. This means three and a half years will have passed, then the next three-and-a-half-year period begins. The Temple mentioned in verses 1 and 2 refers to the one that **will be built in Jerusalem during The Great Tribulation**.

In Rev. 11:3-4 *(3) And I will give power unto my **two witnesses**, and they shall prophesy a thousand two hundred and threescore days, clothed in sackcloth. (4) These are the two olive trees, and the two candlesticks standing before the God of the earth.* God's ***Two Witnesses*** will preach the Truth of God's Word. Let's turn to ***Malachi 4:5*** *Behold, I will send you Elijah the prophet before the coming of the great and dreadful day of the Lord:* One of the two men will be Elijah, the other will possibly be Moses. **Countless Israelites will humbly come to Christ and finally, Redemption will come to Israel!** The Olive Trees & Candlesticks are symbolic of this special spiritual revival.

In Rev. 11:5-6 *(5) And if any man will hurt them, fire proceedeth out of their mouth, and devoureth their enemies: and if any man will hurt them, he must in this manner be killed. (6) These have power to shut heaven, that it rain not in the days of their prophecy: and have power over waters to turn them to blood, and to smite the earth with all plagues, as often as they will.* Perhaps, the two preachers will be *Moses* and *Elijah.* The earthquakes will continue and this will be the beginning of **The Great Tribulation** period. There will be Divine protection for the two witnesses, which God commanded. Therefore, nothing will happen to them until their work on Earth is completed. **They will be given great powers from God.**

In Rev. 11:7-9 *(7) And when they shall have finished their testimony, the beast that ascendeth out of the bottomless pit shall make war against them, and shall overcome them, and kill them. (8) And their dead bodies shall lie in the street of the great city, which spiritually is called Sodom and Egypt, where also our Lord was crucified. (9) And they of the people and kindreds and tongues and nations shall see their dead bodies three days and an half, and shall not suffer their dead bodies to be put in graves.* When their work is completed, means all whom God wants to be Redeemed at that time, will be. Then the Beast ***(Antichrist)*** **will be allowed to kill the two witnesses**. Their dead bodies will be left on display, on the street for three and a half days. Those *Saved* during these several years will be referred to as **"The Tribulation Saints"**.

In Rev. 11:10-13 *(10) And they that dwell upon the earth shall rejoice over them, and make merry, and shall send gifts one to another; because these two prophets tormented them that dwelt on the earth. (11) And after three days and an half the spirit of life from God entered into them, and they stood upon their feet; and great fear fell upon them which saw them. (12) And they heard a great voice from heaven saying unto them, Come up hither. And they ascended up to heaven in a cloud; and their enemies beheld them. (13) And the same hour was there a great earthquake, and the tenth part of the city fell, and in the earthquake were slain of men seven thousand:* ***and <u>the remnant</u> were affrighted, and gave glory to the God of heaven.*** Those unredeemed watching and witnessing such events will be moved to rejoice. They will see the death of the two witnesses. The remainder of **the world will glorify the Antichrist** as the bodies of the two witnesses simply rot. **However, the celebration of the wicked will be short-lived.** The Spirit of God will enter into the bodies and they will stand up and then be lifted into Heaven. Then great fear will fall upon those who have seen this. ***The Remnant*** will give Glory to God, these are *The Tribulation Saints.* Then another great earthquake will take place and a tenth part of the city will fall.

In Rev. 11:14 *(14) The second woe is past; and, behold, the third woe cometh quickly.* The ***second "woe"*** is passed.

In Rev. 11:15 *(15) And the seventh angel sounded; and there were great voices in heaven, saying, The kingdoms of this world are become the kingdoms of our Lord, and of his Christ; and he shall reign for ever and ever.* The ***Seventh Trumpet*** sounds. Great voices from Heaven will be heard on Earth proclaiming Christ will reign forever. This will usher in the 2nd Coming. Then Jesus will defeat His enemies and establish His

Millennial Kingdom on Earth. In **Exodus 15:18** *The Lord shall reign forever and ever.*

In Rev. 11:16 *(16) And the four and twenty elders, which sat before God on their seats, fell upon their faces, and worshipped God.* This signifies The Church will worship The Lord **for all He Is** and for what He has done, is doing, and will do.

In Rev. 11:17 *(17) Saying, We give thee thanks, O Lord God Almighty, which art, and wast, and art to come; because thou hast taken to thee thy great power, and hast reigned.* We will continue to worship Him...

In Rev. 11:18-19 *(18) And the nations were angry, and thy wrath is come, and the time of the dead, that they should be judged, and that thou shouldest give reward unto thy servants the prophets, and to the saints, and them that fear thy name, small and great; and shouldest destroy them which destroy the earth. (19) And the temple of God was opened in heaven, and there was seen in his temple the ark of his testament: and there were lightnings, and voices, and thunderings, and* *an earthquake, and great hail.* The nations will be angry and rebellious. God's Wrath will continue and their eternity in Hell will be secure. Moreover, great hail falls, more lightning, loud voices from Heaven, thundering sounds, and more earthquakes. **God's Wrath will be continuously poured out upon the Earth** towards all rebellious sinful men, women, and children worldwide.

> Pelagianism, Semi-Pelagianism, Open Theism, and ARMINIANISM all have one thing in common, they are each a **FALSE FREEWILL concept of Salvation**, created by man.

Let's turn to **Colossians 2:8 LSB** *See to it that no one takes you captive through* ***philosophy*** *and empty deception, according to* ***the tradition of men,*** *according to the elementary principles of the world, and not according to Christ.* Never "buy into" man's traditions over God's Truths.

> ***"...And as many as were ORDAINED to Eternal Life Believed."***
>
> Acts 13:48

Chapter 12

Commentary *Revelation Chapter 12*

In Rev. 12:1-2 *(1) And there appeared a great wonder in heaven; a woman clothed with the sun, and the moon under her feet, and upon her head a crown of twelve stars: (2) And she being with child cried, travailing in birth, and pained to be delivered.* The woman here is symbolic and represents **Israel,** as portrayed in the Old Testament. **The 12 stars here represent the 12 Tribes of Israel**. Turn to **Genesis 37:9** *And he dreamed yet another dream and told it his brethren, and said, Behold, I have dreamed a dream more; and, behold, the sun and the moon and the eleven stars made obeisance to me.* This was a dream Joseph had; he would be Tribe number twelve. Let's look at verse *(2) the child cried.* **This refers to Israel; it will be waiting and suffering through Satanic Anti-Semitism and constant WARS while waiting for the Messiah.** This is most evident, today.

In Rev. 12:3-4 *(3) And there appeared another wonder in heaven; and behold a great red dragon, having seven heads and ten horns, and seven crowns upon his heads. (4) And his tail drew the third part of the stars of heaven, and did cast them to the earth: and the dragon stood before the woman which was ready to be delivered, for to devour her child as soon as it was born.* The **Red Dragon is no other than Satan**. The color red refers to bloodshed. **The 7 heads and 10 horns are figurative,** they denote the past and future world empires and Satan's control of the world's political affairs. The 1/3 of the stars, refers to the **number of fallen angels** that went with Satan in his rebellion against God. The devouring of her child speaks of Satan's efforts to kill baby Jesus. Let's look at **Matthew 2:13-18**. *(I will capsize)* King Herod sent out his men to kill all the male children in Bethlehem and **surrounding areas from 2 years old and under in an attempt to kill the young boy Jesus**.

In Rev. 12:5-6 *(5) And she brought forth a man child, who was to rule all nations with* *a rod of iron: and her child was caught up unto God, and to his throne. (6) And the woman fled into the wilderness, where she hath a place prepared of God, that they should feed her there a thousand two hundred and threescore days.* The man-child is Jesus. **When Jesus returns, He will rule with a rod of iron**. The child caught up refers to the Ascension *(Acts 1:9)* of Jesus into the clouds. The woman *(Israel)* will flee, this refers to God's protection over those who will heed the warning back in **Daniel 9:27.** Consequently, many Jews will flee for their lives. This all happens in the 2nd half of The Tribulation period; **The Great Tribulation.**

The Antichrist sets up the **Abomination of Desolation**. Let's visit **Matthew 24:15-16** *(15) When ye therefore shall see the* ***abomination of desolation****, spoken of by Daniel the prophet, stand in the holy place, (whoso readeth, let him understand:) (16) Then let them which be in Judaea flee into the mountains:* This is when The Antichrist will set up an image of himself as god. He will renege on his promises to

Israel. **He will desecrate the Holy Place of Israel and claim to be god himself!** This is **The Abomination of Desolation**. This is a warning that some Jews will heed, to flee to the mountains for refuge and many will.

In Rev. 12:7-8 *(7) And there was war in heaven: Michael and his angels fought against the dragon; and the dragon fought and his angels, (8) And prevailed not; neither was their place found any more in heaven.* **We see that a War will break out in Heaven. The Head Angel, Michael and his Holy Angels go against Satan and his demons, and Michael prevails. Then Satan and his demons will be cast out of Heaven permanently. Hallelujah! Praise The Lord.**

In Rev. 12:9 *(9) And the great dragon was cast out, that old serpent, called the Devil, and Satan, which deceiveth the whole world: he was cast out into the earth, and his angels were cast out with him.* We now see Satan will be cast out of Heaven with all his demons. We learn Satan and his demons will still have access to Heaven up to this future point in time. **Today, Satan is seeking whom he may devour on Earth.** He also has control and influence in the hearts of those not Born Again by God. Satan *(the Devil, Lucifer)* is *"The prince of the power of the air"*.

In Rev. 12:10 *(10) And I heard a loud voice saying in heaven, Now is come salvation, and strength, and the kingdom of our God, and the power of his Christ: for the accuser of our brethren is cast down, which accused them before our God, day and night.* **This will be declared loudly, that the Dragon *(Satan)* will be cast out of Heaven forever.** However, Satan will continue to create great damage on Earth during The Great Tribulation. This will include all that God allows him to do. Satan was used by God throughout history to do His Bidding. More on him later…

In Rev. 12:11 *(11) And they overcame him by the blood of the Lamb, and by the word of their testimony; and they loved not their lives unto the death.* This is the same way you and I were or will be saved.

In Rev. 12:12 *(12) Therefore rejoice, ye heavens, and ye that dwell in them.* ***Woe*** *to the inhabiters of the earth and of the sea! for the devil is come down unto you, having great wrath, because he knoweth that he hath but a short time.* The ***third "woe"*** concerns Satan and his demons, their time is limited. They will **cause great savagery** on Earth.

In Rev. 12:13 *(13) And when the dragon saw that he was cast unto the earth, he persecuted the woman which brought forth the man child.* **Satan will focus his destruction particularly on those in the nation of Israel, the birthplace of Jesus.** He can only be in one place at a time.

In Rev. 12:14 *(14) And to the woman were given two wings of a great eagle, that she might fly into the wilderness, into her place, where she is nourished for a time, and times, and half a time, from the face of the serpent.* This is not speaking of a bird's wings but a graphic depiction showing **God's protection of Israel.** This protection will be for the time remaining until The 2nd Coming.

In Rev. 12:15 *(15) And the serpent cast out of his mouth water as a flood after the woman, that he might cause her to be carried away of the flood.* The flood could be literal or figurative here. This could mean a great army or another supernatural catastrophe *(flood)* that Satan will launch toward Israel.

In Rev. 12:16 *(16) And the earth helped the woman, and the earth opened her mouth, and swallowed up the flood which the dragon cast out of his mouth.* This is to say God will open the Earth to swallow up the water or army, therefore, preserving Israel.

In Rev. 12:17 *(17) And the dragon was wroth with the woman, and went to make war with the remnant of her seed, which keep the commandments of God, and have the testimony of Jesus Christ.* **The Dragon *(Satan)* will set out to destroy Israel.**

Turn to **Zechariah 13:9** *And I will bring the third part through the fire, and will refine them as silver is refined, and will try them as gold is tried: they shall call on my name, and I will hear them: I will say, It is my people:*

and they shall say, The Lord is my God. At this future time, God is saying that **HE will bring one-third of all the Israelites to Him.** God says they are HIS People and **they will finally bow to worship Jesus as Christ *(Messiah)*.** Look at **Jeremiah 24:7** *And I will give them a heart to know me, that I am the Lord: and they shall be my people, and I will be their God: for they shall return unto me with their whole heart.* Let's visit **Proverbs 28:14 ESV** *Blessed is the one who fears the Lord always, but whoever hardens his heart will fall into calamity.* **Yet, to fear God is to obey Him.** It's one thing to ***believe in God*** and another thing to ***Believe God.***

"Jesus didn't die to give YOU what YOU want, but to give YOU a heart that wants ONLY HIM."

Joseph Malara, *Theologian*

"We are never free. Everybody in the world tonight is either the Slave of SIN and Satan or else the Slave of Jesus Christ."

Martyn Lloyd Jones, *Pastor*

Chapter 13

Commentary *Revelation Chapter 13*

In Rev. 13:1 *(1) And I stood upon the sand of the sea, and saw a beast rise up out of the sea, having seven heads and ten horns, and upon his horns ten crowns, and upon his heads the name of blasphemy.* We see Satan will draw out of the sea a powerful demon, who will enter into the blasphemous Antichrist; the world's final dictator. **The 7 heads and horns are a representation of power over the world's territories. The crowns stand for ten kings concerning the world's dominion.** This will be a time when God allows Satan to have a field day for the next 3 ½ years. When it says upon his head the name blasphemy; this stands for the fact that the Antichrist will say he is equal to God. He will also profess to be god; which is the ultimate form of blasphemy.

In Rev. 13:2 *(2) And the beast which I saw was like unto a leopard, and his feet were as the feet of a bear, and his mouth as* *the mouth of a lion: and the dragon gave him his power, and his seat, and great authority.* The leopard stands as a metaphor for Greece *(Europe).* The "feet of a bear" is yet another metaphor for Media-Persia *(Iran).* The lion is another metaphor for the Babylonian empire *(Iraq).* The dragon is Satan who will give them great power and authority.

In Rev. 13:3 *(3) And I saw one of his heads as it were wounded to death; and his deadly wound was healed: and all the world wondered after the beast.* This means the **Antichrist** will appear dead and rise from his fake death. This will further deceive the world into believing he is "god".

In Rev. 13:4 *(4) And they worshipped the dragon which gave power unto the beast: and they worshipped the beast, saying, Who is like unto the beast? who is able to make war with him*? Then the **world** will worship the Antichrist as "god", but he will be only a counterfeit, their false idol.

In Rev. 13:5 *(5) And there was given unto him a mouth speaking great things and* *blasphemies; and power was given unto him to continue forty and two months.* The Antichrist will be a gifted liberal speaker and full of charisma. **He will offer false promises with a noble smile of certainty**. God will allow him to continue his reign for The Great Tribulation's remaining time…

In Rev. 13:6 *(6) And he opened his mouth in blasphemy against God, to blaspheme his name, and his tabernacle, and them that dwell in heaven.* We see that the Antichrist will curse Jesus and His *Church* which is in Heaven. He will curse all those in Heaven including the angels, and curse God Almighty. **Thank God "The Church" will no longer be on Earth in that future time! Thank You, Lord!**

In Rev. 13:7 *(7) And it was given unto him to make war with the saints, and to overcome them: and power was given him over all kindreds, and tongues, and nations.* There will be a remnant of newly *Born Again Believers* worldwide. They will be Saved after the Rapture, during The Tribulation. This is not The *Church;* we were raptured 3 ½ years earlier. These future New Believers ***(Tribulation Saints)*** will be massacred both Jews and Gentiles suffering martyrdom.

In Rev. 13:8 *(8) And all that dwell upon the earth shall worship him, whose names are not written in the book of life of the Lamb slain from the foundation of the world.* Quoting, Charles H. Spurgeon, known as (The Prince of Pastors) *"I am glad that my name was written in the Lambs Book of Life before I got here because if God had waited until I got here, He never would have chosen me."* I too can say the same; we all can. Indeed, no one is worthy of Salvation! What amazing Mercy and Grace God has bestowed on many! **Moreover, those Born Again by God *(Elect)* will NOT worship the Antichrist during this forthcoming time.**

In Rev. 13:9-10 *(9) If any man have an ear, let him hear. (10) He that leadeth into captivity shall go into captivity: he that killeth with the sword must be killed with the sword. Here is the patience and the faith of the* *saints.* **This will be a plea to God's New Believers *at that time*. This means that during this future time, New Believers should allow themselves to be jailed, tortured, and killed. Specifically, knowing soon they too will be with Jesus.**

In Rev. 13:11-12 *(11) And I beheld another beast coming up out of the earth, and he had two horns like a lamb, and he spake as a dragon. (12) And he exerciseth all the power of the first beast before him, and causeth the earth and them which dwell therein to worship the first beast, whose deadly wound was healed.* **This other beast will be the False Prophet.** Many including me believe he will be from the Roman Catholic "Church". He will be a **helper** to the Antichrist. He will display his total alliance with the Antichrist and both will be under the power of Satan. Likewise, all unbelievers **work for their daddy Satan**, knowingly or unknowingly. We are **all** children of Satan at conception *(conceived in sin)* and remain this way, *(Damned; under a curse)* **unless Born Again by God.**

In Rev. 13:13 *(13) And he doeth great wonders so that he maketh fire come down from heaven on the earth in the sight of men,* The False Prophet will perform great miracles and all but God's Elect will be greatly misled.

In Rev. 13:14 *(14) And deceiveth them that dwell on the earth by the means of those miracles which he had power to do in the sight of the beast; saying to them that dwell on the earth, that they should make an image to the beast, which had the wound by a sword, and did live.* This verse describes the **image** of The **Antichrist** *(Beast),* which will be created and used to deceive the people.

In Rev. 13:15 *(15) And he had power to give life unto the image of the beast, that the image of the beast should both speak, and cause that as many as would not worship the image of the beast should be killed.* There will be a reproduction of the Antichrist *(possibly a sculpture)* that will be erected during the **Abomination of Desolation**. This will happen in the Jerusalem Temple. The **False Prophet** will make the image seem to talk.

This **False Prophet** will be using signs and wonders *(even artificial intelligence, AI).* He will set out to prove The Antichrist is god. He will be devoted to control and destruction. **Those who will not believe and won't worship The Antichrist will be KILLED!**

In Rev. 13:16 *(16) And he causeth all, both small and great, rich and poor, free and bond, to receive a mark in their right hand, or in their forehead.* **This is the beginning of taking an identifying MARK**. Perhaps, a tattoo *(barcode;* ***tracking all personal*** *info).* **It will be a visible symbol on the hand or forehead** of all the people left in the world, those rich and poor, and those even in prisons. **This will happen after 3 years into The Tribulation.**

In Rev. 13:17 *(17) And that no man might buy or sell, save he that had the mark, or the name of the beast, or the number of his name.* The One-World Government will be under the guidance of The Antichrist; he will create an **openly identifying mark**. This will further divide those who do not worship the

Antichrist from those who do. The **Mark of The Beast** will only allow those individuals with it to buy personal necessities like food, gas, and water. **Consequently, all others without this MARK will be criminal outcasts and sought after to be KILLED.** If you say you don't have any enemies, you don't know Jesus. **2 Timothy 3:12** *Yea, and* ***all*** *that will live godly* ***in Christ*** *Jesus* ***shall suffer persecution***. The 1st things to go for a True Believer, will be family and friends, then this wicked alluring world. **It will cost you everything to be a True Believer.** Amen.

> **"What the natural man needs first and foremost is not education or reformation, but life. It is because the sinner is DEAD that he needs to be Born Again."**
>
> A.W. Pink, *Bible Teacher*

In Rev. 13:18 *(18) Here is wisdom. Let him that hath understanding count the number of the beast: for it is the number of a* *man; and his number is Six hundred threescore and six.* This number **666** will **then *(not now)*** identify the man called The **Antichrist**. However, this number has many today speculating as to who it will be. It is far-fetched to even assume who it will be. Moreover, **those living in that future time will know**. We know the number 6 falls short of God's number of perfection being 7. The answer may remain a mystery up until the time of The Tribulation. Furthermore, I and all other Believers will be with Jesus before the Tribulation begins. We should not be concerned with this matter or speculate past what God says in His Word, to do so is futile.

"In life, there are two paths, one of wickedness in you and one of Righteousness IN HIM."

Joseph Malara, *Theologian*

"If a person has no genuine interest in GOD today, why would he or she want to spend eternity with GOD?"

Joseph Malara, *Theologian*

Why isn't America in the Bible?

The current trend in America speaks volumes concerning its future downfall. America is under God's Judgment. **Today America** is the last nation to succumb to total apostasy, a Nation founded on Judeo-Christian values from God's Holy Word. Undoubtedly, even our freedom of speech has come to an end. Today in America, if one speaks of Biblical values publicly, they can lose their livelihood, be threatened, harassed, and even be physically attacked or incarcerated.

Today Biblical Truths are considered "Hate Speech", even praying in the name of Jesus is called harassment. The world like America, only wants cults and counterfeits. This is evident due to widespread dishonesty, and collusion with toxic leftist *(worldliness)* platform policies that are intolerant of God's values. This is today's Godless Democratic Socialist Party. **America will soon become just another 3rd world nation, in EXTREME DEBT with countless**

illegal immigrants creating chaos. America's tax dollars support these immigrants. America doesn't take care of its citizens first; any country will fall when this happens. **This "fall" will happen very soon after the Rapture.** Perhaps another way this could happen is because of Democratic military weakness; China, Russia, Iran, and other Nations may simultaneously launch nuclear or even conventional weapons to abolish America. **Those alive would yield to whoever was in power or voted into power then. The Antichrist would call for world peace at this future time.**

America is a Constitutional Republic and the Antichrist changes all that into a Totalitarian Dictatorship. America will embrace it; this effort has already manifested itself in today's Democratic Party. The Left has created a misnomer, by gaslighting all those who oppose them, labeling them radical right-wing extremists, religious extremists, and Nationalists, and even comparing them to Neo-Nazis. The Left uses continuous mass media disinformation and misinformation. They use unchecked "facts" with collaborated concealed corruption involving the *FBI*, *NSA*, and *CIA*. We already have a weaponized two-tiered biased Justice System that favors the Globalist Agenda! The Left is now trying to imprison their political opponents just like in a *banana republic*. This is evident concerning President Trump in 2024, who was convicted in a sham trial on 34 phony felony counts.

All real news, *(conservative viewpoints)* **THE TRUTH will be silenced and taken off the air permanently.** This would include radio, social media, cell phones, and TV, which are all avenues of communication. There will only be Networks and news outlets saying what the Antichrist wants everyone to hear, believe, and side with. The Antichrist will birth countless lies, misinformation, disinformation, and the **normalization of perversions**. The left will use liberal open-border policies, corruption, travesties, inept leadership, greed, pride, and countless diabolical strategies to bring bankruptcy to America and its citizens. Americans will max out their credit cards and empty their bank accounts just to buy food and essentials to stay alive. **Those trying to hold on to right over wrong**; those who won't bend to the current culture of evil and perversion will suffer greatly. Many today wanting real justice are treated similarly to the ones who will NOT take the Mark of the Beast and therefore will be sought out to be slaughtered. Let's look at **Genesis 6:5** *And God saw that the wickedness of man was great in the earth, and that every imagination of the thoughts of his heart was only evil continually.* **This is when God decided to flood the Earth and kill Millions and Millions of men, women, and children.** He only spared Noah and his family. This is where we are today in the eyes of God according to His Word.

Consequently, after the Rapture, when all of God's People and the Holy Spirit in them are gone, then **America will ALSO go against Israel and side with Satan.** I sadly see that happening even as I write concerning the Israel-Hamas War. Israel was brutally attacked on October 7, 2024, by Hamas and as a result, many have bought into anti-Semitism! The next generation of college-aged students is in support of Hamas and not Israel. They are advocates for the termination of Israel, chanting “From the River to the Sea”. Democrats have pushed and passed new laws of evil unyielding wicked perversions, legalizing abominations that are intolerant to morality all under the guise of (DEI) *Diversity, Equity, Inclusion, Equality,* and *Protecting LGBTQ+ Minorities.*

It is clear to see which direction America is moving. We are the only Nation that funds its own demise. We do this by giving our tax dollars away to support other nations' wars and fund both sides. However, we have countless veterans and homeless people right here in America; but we chose to help our enemies over our allies. Democrats are crooked and have their own rules which make no sense. They include “kickbacks”, money, favors, and more power “under the table” aka “back door deals” to them, their friends, and family if they vote a certain way.

Those who love *(the root of all evil)* large amounts of MONEY *(cash, or $ in offshore bank accounts)*, will lie, cheat, steal, and kill. American Democratic cities with their overwhelming dishonesty would rather protect the criminal over the victim and even make criminals heroes. **The corruption coming from the *Deep State* is apparent and expressed loudly, pridefully, and boldly. They are screaming,** "We won't give up our control of power, we will cheat, riot, steal, kill, or imprison anyone who comes against us." **These are all visible birth pains of the Rapture...** *(Pages 26, 158-163, 197-200)*

Finally, a Poetry book with Biblical Truths, online everywhere even on Amazon! **"God's Clarity Through Poetry 2"**

Chapter 14

Commentary *Revelation Chapter 14*

In Rev. 14:1 *(1) And I looked, and, lo, a Lamb stood on the mount Sion, and with him a hundred forty and four thousand, having his Father's name written in their foreheads.* This speaks of The Lamb ***(Jesus)***. He will literally return to **Mount Zion** and the **ground will split;** this is in the city of Jerusalem. The one hundred and forty-four thousand **(144,000)** will be with Him. Those with God's MARK (not the same as the Mark of the beast) on their foreheads came through The Tribulation. This verse speaks of **His 2nd Coming.** This will come to fruition in chapter 19.

In Rev. 14:2 *(2) And I heard a voice from heaven, as the voice of many waters, and as the voice of a great thunder: and I heard the voice of harpers harping with their harps:* The Apostle John recounts what he hears, then **Father God** will Speak from Heaven. He will be heard down on Earth. There will also be harps playing in a way that we have never heard, making beautiful music.

In Rev. 14:3 *(3) And they sung as it were a new song before the throne, and before the four beasts, and the elders: and no man could learn that song but the hundred and forty and four thousand, which were redeemed from the earth.* There will be a NEW song that only the 144,000 would know. They will all sing that song of redemption.

In Rev. 14:4 *(4) These are they which were not defiled with women; for they are virgins. These are they which follow the Lamb whithersoever he goeth. These were redeemed from among men, being the firstfruits unto God and to the Lamb.* This refers to all of the 144,000 redeemed Jewish evangelists. They will have all resisted the evil and sexually perverse illicit system of The Antichrist. They will resist all false gospels and remain steadfast in God's Truths obediently. These men are the Old Testament *(first fruits)*, the first large group of Redeemed Israel. They will be used for special purposes by God.

In Rev. 14:5 *(5) And in their mouth was found no guile: for they are without fault before the throne of God.* These men will represent God's Truths accurately. They will each be a bold truth-teller and loyal without exception. We should all want to be as such.

In Rev. 14:6 *(6) And I saw another angel fly in the midst of heaven, having the everlasting gospel to preach unto them that dwell on the earth, and to every nation, and kindred, and tongue, and people.* God will send down **an angel** to **preach the Gospel** to those who have an ear to hear. This will be before God purges the world of all evil.

In Rev. 14:7 *(7) Saying with a loud voice, Fear God, and give glory to him; for the hour of his judgment is come: and worship him that made heaven, and earth, and the sea, and the fountains of waters.* Their end is very near. The world is told to **FEAR GOD, not Satan, or The Antichrist, or his minions**. The world is told one last time to

worship and give glory to the Living God who created all things.

In Rev. 14:8 *(8) And there followed another angel, saying, Babylon is fallen, is fallen, that great city, because she made all nations drink of the wine of the wrath of her fornication.* God will send a **second angel**, seemingly nothing came from the first. The word **"Babylon"** here is used figuratively and refers to the ***whole world system*** of *Idolatry, Immorality*, and *Blasphemy*. This system comprises the Earth's gross number of sexual perversions, including the absence of moral, political, social, and academic values. **They are all absent of God's Standards.** These **sins** are widely exposed and increase daily worldwide, as I write.

In Rev. 14:9 *(9) And the third angel followed them, saying with a loud voice, If any man worship the beast and his image, and receive his mark in his forehead, or in his hand*, There will be a **third angel** who will give God's warning to those on Earth at that time. The third angel brings with him a dreadful warning for **whosoever takes the MARK** of The Antichrist, *(Beast).*

In Rev. 14:10 *(10) The same shall drink of the wine of the wrath of God, which is poured out without mixture into the cup of his indignation; and he shall be tormented with fire and brimstone in the presence of the holy angels, and in the presence of the Lamb:* Those who will take the **Mark of The Beast** will suffer the consequences of God's Wrath. Namely, in their remaining days on Earth, then everlasting Hell. It would be far better if such a person were never born.

In Rev. 14:11 *(11) And the smoke of their torment ascendeth up for ever and ever: and they have no rest day nor night, who worship the beast and his image, and whosoever receiveth the mark of his name.* **This verse talks of everlasting Hell, The Lake of Fire.**

In Rev. 14:12 *(12) Here is the patience of the saints: here are they that keep the commandments of God, and the faith of Jesus.* This is visible evidence of the

Perseverance of the Saints. This is solely because of His supernatural Gift of **Effectual Faith** given to God's Elect, **Not One will be lost.** God's Grace gives us the ability to abide by His Commandments. His yoke is easy; His love everlasting. Let's visit **Ephesians 2:8-9** *(8) For by grace are ye saved through faith; and that* ***not*** *of yourselves: it is the* ***gift of God****: (9) Not of works, lest any man should boast*. **This again means Salvation is ALL of God and none of man.** He Lives in His Elect) and we boast of Him.

In Rev. 14:13 *(13) And I heard a voice from heaven saying unto me, Write, Blessed are the dead which die* ***in the Lord*** *from henceforth: Yea, saith the Spirit, that they may rest from their labours; and their works do follow them.* The Apostle John continues to write what he sees. There will be rewards in Heaven. **Those who are martyred for Christ's sake *(In Christ)* will be rewarded by Christ Personally.**

There will also come a day when **ALL believers will be judged.** Let's look at

2 Corinthians 5:10 *For we must* ***all*** *appear before the judgment seat of Christ; that every one may receive the things done in his body, according to that he hath done, whether it be good or bad.* This **Judgment Seat of Christ** is also known as the **"Bema Seat".** This means *(a raised platform)* before Christ. There each ***(Believer)*** will be judged on all things he or she has done good and bad. This judgment does not concern one's salvation, since this Judgment is only for God's Elect. **This will concern our Faithful Accountability, Works, Responsibility, and Obedience to Christ and His Word.**

There will be eternal rewards from Jesus Himself. These rewards will be handed out to those He deems worthy. **This will be based on us and how we represented Him in HIS TRUTH during our time on Earth, once Saved by God.** First of all, in your life make sure that all your "good deeds" **point people to God, The Author of those good deeds!** Let's turn to **2 Timothy 4:7-8.** Here we read what The Apostle Paul is proclaiming: ***I have fought a good fight, I***

have finished my course, I have kept the faith: Henceforth there is laid up for me a crown of righteousness, which the Lord, the righteous judge, shall give me at that day: and not to me only, but unto all them also that love his appearing.

I had a dear Believing best friend of mine named Dan. **He would always say, *"I don't want God mad at me"* and lived his life accordingly.** I would say, "Hey Dan let's have lunch tomorrow at 1 pm" and he would reply, "I can't say for sure, are you trying to make me a liar?" He had the **fear** of The Lord in his heart and the **highest reverence** for God. My dear friend Dan passed away much, much too young. I miss him dearly, but I do believe I will see him in Heaven one day.

Let's look at **Philippians 2:12** *Wherefore, my beloved, as ye have always obeyed, not as in my presence only, but now much more in my absence, work out your own salvation with fear and trembling.* This is to say, since you know through God's Word that you are His, Born Again; **bring what's**

in you to the surface, live out and exhibit Christ in you! This exemplifies and is a witness to who the Holy Spirit within you has transformed you into, **a New Creation!** Overall, such a person only desires God's Truths, not the lies and false opinions of this world. **We must be obedient and allow His Word to change us;** this is the process of **Sanctification**, while simultaneously upholding a Holy Terror and the Deepest **Reverence for God**. We must also be **responsible** and **accountable** for all our actions and inactions, in front of a Holy and Righteous God **who lives in us**.

Let's look at **Proverbs 1:7** *The fear of the Lord is the beginning of knowledge: but fools despise wisdom and instruction.*

"If we are HIS, we love HIM and would want to be obedient unto death."

Joseph Malara, *Theologian*

"IT'S ALL SUBJECT TO GOD'S WORD"

In Rev. 14:14 *(14) And I looked, and behold a white cloud, and upon the cloud one sat like unto the Son of man, having on his head a golden crown, and in his hand a sharp sickle.* John, sees Jesus wearing a Crown on His Head which signifies His Greatness; in His Hand is a sharp sickle, which is figurative of His swift and devastating **Righteous Judgment**. He will use it to kill His enemies, those who love this world more than Him.

In Rev. 14:15 *(15) And another angel came out of the temple, crying with a loud voice to him that sat on the cloud, Thrust in thy sickle, and reap: for the time is come for thee to reap; for the harvest of the earth is ripe.* This is speaking of the **ungodly people of the world** *(harvest of the earth).* They will at that point be gathered up and judged. This signifies the near end.

In Rev. 14:16 *(16) And he that sat on the cloud thrust in his sickle on the earth, and the earth was reaped.* **This signifies God's Judgment upon the people of the Earth.**

In Rev. 14:17 *(17) And another angel came out of the temple which is in heaven, he also having a sharp sickle.* This refers to God's Judgment which will continue with an angel to assist Jesus.

In Rev. 14:18-20 *(18) And another angel came out from the altar, which had power over fire; and cried with a loud cry to him that had the sharp sickle, saying, Thrust in thy sharp sickle, and gather the clusters of the vine of the earth; for her grapes are fully ripe. (19) And the angel thrust in his sickle into the earth, and gathered the vine of the earth, and cast it into the great winepress of the wrath of God. (20) And the winepress was trodden without the city, and blood came out of the winepress, even unto the horse bridles, by the space of a thousand and six hundred furlongs.* Then another angel will come and he will represent the prayers of the Saints. He is associated with the burning fire at Heaven's Altar. This will be the **War at Armageddon** the final decisive battle against all of God's enemies. It will encompass 180 miles between Palestine to Southwest

Jordan. God wants it outside of Jerusalem. There will be a bloodbath of horror. This is signified by the imagery of grapes in a wine press, indicating the amount of bloodshed that will incur.

"God Saved you FOR HIMSELF; God Saved you BY HIMSELF; God Saved you FROM HIMSELF."

Paul Washer, *Pastor - Evangelist*

"Today false preachers tell people what they want to hear and people love them! The true Prophets and Apostles told People what they needed to hear and they were stoned and killed. Christians will be HATED."

Joseph Malara, *Theologian*

2 Timothy 3:16

ALL scripture is given by inspiration of God, and is profitable for doctrine, for reproof, for correction, for instruction in righteousness

Chapter 15

Commentary *Revelation Chapter 15*

In Rev. 15:1 *(1) And I saw another sign in heaven, great and marvellous, seven angels having the seven last plagues; for in them is filled up the wrath of God.* These will be God's final judgments at the end of the 7 years of Tribulation. **This will be all God's Wrath,** this will **not** come from Satan, or the False Prophet, or The Antichrist. **The "Seal", "Trumpet" and "woe" Judgments have all been completed. The "Bowl *(Vial)* Judgments" will now commence in swift order.**

In Rev. 15:2 *(2) And I saw as it were a sea of glass mingled with fire: and them that had gotten the victory over the beast, and over his image, and over his mark, and over the number of his name, stand on the sea of glass, having the harps of God.* God's Throne is stationed on a clear glass-like gold pavement. **We see those who will refuse to take the MARK. They will be jailed, tortured, or killed for not doing so.**

However, they will be rewarded for their victory over The Antichrist.

In Rev. 15:3 *(3) And they sing the song of Moses the servant of God, and the song of the Lamb, saying, Great and marvellous are thy works, Lord God Almighty; just and true are thy ways, thou King of saints.* These martyrs will sing the song of Moses *(Exodus 15).* This song was sung as the Israelites passed through the open Red Sea on dry ground when they escaped Pharaoh's Egyptian army. Consequently, Pharaoh's army drowned when God closed back up the sea, once His People *(Israelites)* were safe on dry ground. *(Exodus 14:13-31)*

In Rev. 15:4 *(4) Who shall not fear thee, O Lord, and glorify thy name? for thou only art holy: for all nations shall come and worship before thee; for thy judgments are made manifest.* We know that God is Holy, Just, and Righteous, likewise, all of God's Elect from every nation and tongue will profess the same. **He is Worthy of all our praise and worship, at all times.**

In Rev. 15:5 *(5) And after that I looked, and, behold, the temple of the tabernacle of the testimony in heaven was opened:* The Apostle John has seen the dwelling place of God. We do not see the "Church" because **God is dealing with Redeemed Israel**.

In Rev. 15:6 *(6) And the seven angels came out of the temple, having the seven plagues, clothed in pure and white linen, and having their breasts girded with golden girdles.* These will be the final judgments from God. The angels are of unblemished glory and pure.

In Rev. 15:7 *(7) And one of the four beasts gave unto the seven angels seven golden vials full of the wrath of God, who liveth for ever and ever.* At this time God will again pour out His Righteous Wrath.

In Rev. 15:8 *(8) And the temple was filled with smoke from the glory of God, and from his power; and no man was able to enter into the temple, till the seven plagues of the seven angels were fulfilled.* God's Wrath must pass before anyone would be able to enter into His Holy of Holies.

The number "seven" of plagues is significant and always means God's Completion or Perfection.

"The only one who can produce genuine repentance in your soul is GOD."

R.C. Sproul, *Pastor-Theologian*

"Any decision towards Salvation is again all God's before He created this world and no one can decide to follow Jesus, but His Children can agree to obey Him more and more each day. No one can invite Jesus into a heart, He gives new hearts to His Children without asking for their approval, permission, consent, or knowledge, and in His Time not yours, if at all."

Joseph Malara, *Theologian*

"Digging Deeper into God's Truth Defines a Christian"

Chapter 16

Commentary *Revelation Chapter 16*

In Rev. 16:1 *(1) And I heard a great voice out of the temple saying to the seven angels, Go your ways, and pour out the vials of the wrath of God upon the earth.* The beginning of the end is Commanded by God. **This Divine catastrophe will be all orchestrated, planned, and carried out by God.**

In Rev. 16:2 *(2) And the first went, and poured out his vial upon the earth, and there fell a noisome and grievous sore upon the men which had the mark of the beast, and upon them which worshipped his image.* The ***First Bowl*** is poured out upon the Earth. It is best described as a **type of leprosy** but it will be much worse. This will be for **everyone who has the MARK of the beast** on their forehead or hand at that time.

In Rev. 16:3 *(3) And the second angel poured out his vial upon the sea, and it became as the blood of a dead man: and* *every living soul died in the sea.* The ***Second Bowl*** is poured out upon the sea. **Then everything living in the sea will die.** This will also include both man, mammals and all marine life. **The whole sea waters will become the blood of a *dead man*.**

In Rev. 16:4 *(4) And the third angel poured out his vial upon the rivers and fountains of waters, and they became blood.* The third angel poured The ***Third Bowl.*** Then all the rivers and freshwater **supply will become blood**.

In Rev. 16:5 *(5) And I heard the angel of the waters say, Thou art righteous, O Lord, which art, and wast, and shalt be, because thou hast judged thus.* This will be glorifying God for Who He Is, the Sovereign Lord. He is over all things from eternity past, present, and eternity future.

In Rev. 16:6 *(6) For they have shed the blood of saints and prophets, and thou hast given them blood to drink; for they are worthy.* **God's Judgment will be poetic justice with vengeance.** Those being judged had made martyrs of God's Chosen People. They will have nothing to drink but the blood which they have spilled. **This is called righteous indignation aka God's Vengeance.**

In Rev. 16:7 *(7) And I heard another out of the altar say, Even so, Lord God Almighty, true and righteous are thy judgments.* This will be yet another reinforcement confirming God's Judgments. **His Wrath will all be Justified and fully Righteous towards those who deny Him.**

In Rev. 16:8 *(8) And the fourth angel poured out his vial upon the sun, and power was given unto him to scorch men with fire.* The ***Fourth Bowl*** describes more **heat that will be poured down** onto Earth's unconverted *(unredeemed)* populations. The Earth will already be in dire ruins. However, God's Righteous Anger will continue.

In Rev. 16:9 *(9) And men were scorched with great heat, and blasphemed the name of God, which hath power over these plagues: and they* ***repented not*** *to give* *him glory*. The remaining **people will curse God** and refuse to repent *(no change of mind).* **Those believing in a false jesus will always reject The Biblical Jesus.** Those still alive will **refuse** to glorify God, even with His great power on full display! There will be countless people paying for their sins in Hell. The oceans will rise due to melting ice caps caused by the excessive heat. There will be greater and greater loss of life.

In Rev. 16:10 *(10) And the fifth angel poured out his vial upon the seat of the beast; and his kingdom was full of darkness, and they gnawed their tongues for pain.* The ***Fifth Bowl*** refers to Satan's rule. This will limit the Antichrist and the False Prophets' control. **Their power will then be darkened and restricted**. Moreover, there will be continued intense pain worldwide.

In Rev. 16:11 *(11) And blasphemed the God of heaven because of their pains and their sores, and repented not of their deeds.* This will be the response to God's Wrath; they will curse Him more! **This is what**

today's movies do constantly. They use God's Name and the Lord's Name as curse words! This only shows the world will still have its trust in itself, also in the deceitful and wicked Antichrist and NOT in the God of Heaven, not in the Biblical Jesus.

In Rev. 16:12 *(12) And the sixth angel poured out his vial upon the great river Euphrates; and the water thereof was dried up, that the way of the kings of the east might be prepared.* The ***Sixth Bowl*** speaks of the start of the **WAR OF ARMAGEDDON** *(Megiddo a city in northern Israel).* This is where great armies will gather for this final battle. God will supernaturally dry up the "Great River Euphrates" aka "The Great River" to make a way for the East to reach and battle Israel. This final war with Israel is under *"birth pains"* even as I write. However, this will all occur **after 3 ½ years into The Tribulation.** This war is not a single battle but a war lasting approximately 3 ½ years until the return of Jesus. Let's turn to **Genesis 15:18** *In the same day the Lord made a covenant with Abram, saying, Unto* *thy seed have I given this land, from the river of Egypt unto the great river, the river Euphrates*: Here we see that God has promised this land to **belong to Israel. I believe that Israel has been cheated out of its original lands promised to Abraham** aka "Abram". Israel, Biblically owns the **"Land of Canaan"** *(West Bank and the Gaza Strip, Jordan, and the southern portions of Syria and Lebanon)*, the Promised Land. This also refers to **"The Holy Land"** *(located between the Mediterranean Sea and the eastern bank of the Jordan River including Palestine, and Jerusalem).*

In Rev. 16:13 *(13) And I saw three unclean spirits like frogs come out of the mouth of the dragon, and out of the mouth of the beast, and out of the mouth of the false prophet.* This is speaking of demonic activity and mentions **the "Dragon" or Satan; The "Beast" or Antichrist. Also, "The False Prophet", who is loyal to The Antichrist.**

In Rev. 16:14 *(14) For they are the* ***spirits of devils, working miracles****, which* *go forth unto the kings of the earth and of the whole world, to gather them to the battle of that great day of God Almighty.* We see supernatural miracles will be created by demons or Satan himself.

This mayhem and **satanic miracles will deceive** the pagan "Kings" *(the world's remaining powers).* This is regarding Russia, the Middle East, and other **Anti-Semitic nations.** They will all move and come together to try and destroy Israel. **The evil trio *(Satan, the Antichrist, and the False Prophet)*** will use whatever false propaganda they need by convincing the whole world to hate and come against Israel. **The Lord Jesus and no one else could stop the little nation of Israel from being devastated.** This is evident, even now.

In Rev. 16:15 *(15) Behold, I come as a thief.* ***Blessed is he that watcheth****, and keepeth his garments, lest he walk naked, and they see his shame.* He is not speaking of His Church; we will already be in Heaven. Jesus is proclaiming what those few followers alive during this time must know. Today, we need to be reminded of this frequently; **be ready as *watchmen* for His Return! This warning would also include being ready for eternity, *one's death***. We notice this warning was spoken of in a few passages. Let's look at **2 Peter 3:10** *But the day of the Lord will come as a thief in the night; in the which the heavens shall pass away with a great noise, and the elements shall melt with fervent heat, the earth also and the works that are therein shall be burned up*. First, The Lord returns *(The 2nd Coming)* and then the rest of this verse will happen in His timing.

In Rev. 16:16 *(16) And he gathered them together into a place called in the Hebrew tongue* ***Armageddon.*** This is a large area in northern Israel called **"Mount Megiddo"**. This is where the current-day Kibbutz is located. This is the location that will encounter the **Last Battle on Earth** with all its remaining armies.

It's called the **War of Armageddon**. It is mentioned only once in the Bible. This battle will be described in the later part of Revelation chapter 19 it will encompass most of Israel. It will comprise all **Anti-Semitic nations,** all those against Israel.

In Rev. 16:17 *(17) And the seventh angel poured out his vial into the air; and there came a great voice out of the temple of heaven, from the throne, saying, It is done.* The ***Seventh Bowl*** is poured out. This will signify the near completion of God's Wrath toward Earth; for the time being, the voice of God will proclaim, "IT IS DONE!"

In Rev. 16:18-19 *(18) And there were voices, and thunders, and lightnings; and there was a great earthquake, such as was not since men were upon the earth, so mighty an earthquake, and so great. (19) And the great city was divided into three parts, and the cities of the nations fell: and great Babylon came in remembrance before God, to give unto her the cup of the wine of the fierceness of his wrath.* We can see that God will create a massive earthquake that will split The Great City *(Israel)* into 3 parts. **God will give Babylon *(Iraq or Rome)*, possibly the home of The Antichrist, a hefty dose of His ferocity!**

All the cities of each nation worldwide will fall to complete ruin. Let us now turn to **Isaiah 13:6,9** *(6) Howl ye; for the day of the Lord is at hand; it shall come as a destruction from the Almighty. (9) Behold, the day of the Lord cometh, cruel both with wrath and fierce anger, to lay the land desolate: and he shall destroy the sinners thereof out of it.* **This couldn't be any clearer, The 2nd Coming.**

In Rev. 16:20 *(20) And every island fled away, and the mountains were not found.* **This describes an unthinkable situation of land separation. There will be completely different topographies.**

In Rev. 16:21 *(21) And there fell upon men a great hail out of heaven, every stone about the weight of a talent: and men blasphemed God because of the plague of the hail; for the plague thereof was exceeding* *great.* The damage will be fearsome as God's Wrath will be unleashed. There will be a great hail *(ice)*; as heavy as a talent or more *(75 pounds each).* They will be dropping on the Earth with fierce power and speed. They will destroy everything and everyone in their path. Nevertheless, those still living only blasphemy *(curse)* God more! **This marks the near end of The Great Tribulation.**

"A Church fed on excitement is no New Testament Church at all. The desire for surface stimulation is a sure mark of the fallen nature, the very thing Christ died to deliver us from."

A.W. Tozer, *Pastor*

"The Heart that has really tasted the Grace of Christ, will instinctively HATE SIN."

J. C. Ryle, *Bishop*

Chapter 17

Commentary *Revelation Chapter 17*

In Rev. 17:1 *(1) And there came one of the seven angels which had the seven vials, and talked with me, saying unto me, Come hither; I will shew unto thee the judgment of the* ***great whore*** *that sitteth upon many waters:* We see The Apostle John being lead through these upcoming events. This is through a Divine Vision. **There won't be any more Divine Judgments beyond the *Seals, Trumpets, Woes,* and *Bowls.*** The *great whore* would include all false religions, and of course, **The World System** at that time. Therefore, it's not limited to "churches" but includes worldwide all those who profess another *jesus*. These false movements would include Pentecostal, Roman Catholic, 7th Day Adventist, Jehovah's Witnesses, Methodist, Mormon, Charismatic, Non-Denominational, and Word of Life "churches" to name a few. This *(great whore)* list includes all religions that reject Jesus as God and reject the Trinity. This includes those not Born Again by God but by their own self-centered and selfish “free will”. These would be included and rightly named the *(great whore)*. However, there will be a *remnant* whom God will save out of those false movements. There are *Tares* mixed in with the *Wheat*, see Matthew 13.

This is worth repeating just in case you too were bamboozled, like I once was. Let’s revisit the “churches” above which are spoken of back in **Revelation 3:16** *So then because thou art lukewarm, and neither cold nor hot, I will spue thee out of my mouth.* We again see Jesus **not** accepting those who are actively religious, those caught up in man's traditions, or any work-based salvational method. Indeed, being simply *(lukewarm)* means not fully committed, like those who could never take Jesus seriously for who He Is, but what He could do for them. Then some are ***antinomians,*** who believe that being obedient to God through Jesus is legalistic. Obedience *(Lordship Salvation)* isn’t legalism, it’s a symptom of True Salvation. However, many bought into a "cheap grace" gospel of "easy believeism", where one simply says they believe! However, there is no Biblical *fruit*, no changed life, and no newfound love for His Word. **They also reject Biblical correction and Biblical Christianity. They have no burden for the souls of the lost.** Many deceptively use online search engines to find God's Truths; **don't!** He is found only in His Word with accurate discernment of it. Let's again see **Matthew 7:22-23** *(22) Many will say to me in that day, Lord, Lord, have we not prophesied in thy name? and in thy name have cast out devils? and in thy name done many wonderful works? (23) And then will I (JESUS) profess unto them, I never knew you: depart from me, ye that work iniquity.* They call Jesus Lord, Lord but were not Born Again *(John 3:3)*.

This unbiblical act is an everyday occurrence. When some so-called "pastor" invites or coerces someone to "get saved", they would lead one to say a "sinners' prayer". The "pastor" may say, walk the aisle, raise your hand, or repeat some prayer. The "pastors" who practice this nonsense and those who have in the past, are themselves **false converts**. They only create more false converts worldwide! **I was a victim of such unbiblical acts and went on to repeat them!** There is no "accepting", "choosing", "inviting", or "deciding" towards one's salvation. Salvation is always 100% GOD and ZERO% man, period. Get a copy of *"Digging Deeper into God's Truth Defines a Christian".* That book will explain **Soteriology** in a way all will understand.

Moreover, every religion that denies **Jesus is God incarnate, is lost.** Those who deny **the Trinity** e.g., Muslim *(Islam),* Buddhism, Hinduism, Agnosticism, New Age, and Judaism again are Hellbound. These above would be added to the combined description of the ***great whore****; as* described in verse one. This will include all who at that time will worship the Antichrist, who accepted the MARK of the Beast and those who bought into his one-world religion. Let's take a look at **1 Corinthians 16:22 LSB** *If anyone does not love the Lord, he is to be* *accursed. Maranatha.* This means all who are not **In Christ** are Hellbound; Come, Lord!

> **"False teachers are the Judgment of God upon a wicked defiled people who although they have knowledge of God they do NOT want Him. And so God sends them the teachers that they themselves desire."**
>
> Paul Washer, *Pastor - Evangelist*

In Rev. 17:2 *(2) With whom the kings of the earth have committed fornication, and the inhabitants of the earth have been made drunk with the wine of her fornication.* This scripture is explaining in a way that we can better understand **idolatry**. The world was, is, and will always be drawn into a false system of religion. This is apparent as I write this book. There are sadly over 4,000 man-made *(Satan-derived)* religions, which are all false. There are also countless false idols of one's own making. However, there is only ONE real Way, The Biblical Jesus. **Most people love this world and their lifestyle more than God.**

In Rev. 17:3 *(3) So he carried me away in the spirit into the wilderness: and I saw a woman sit upon a scarlet-coloured beast, full of names of blasphemy, having seven heads and ten horns.* The angel will carry The Apostle John into the wilderness. He provided a vision of the wealthy, rich and powerful beast ***(Antichrist)***. **He possesses nothing but blasphemy towards God.** The ten horns and seven heads represent his future *temporary* control of the nations and political alliances.

In Rev. 17:4 *(4) And the woman was arrayed in purple and scarlet colour, and decked with gold and precious stones and pearls, having a golden cup in her hand full of abominations and filthiness of her fornication:* This imagery is one of great wealth and prestige with mighty military power as well. **However, this pretty whore *(Babylon)* will be dirty, filthy, and evil, and capable of the deepest betrayal.** Those dressed up like the Pharisees, as in today's Catholic exotic garments show only an outward display of holiness. Let's see what Jesus says in

Matthew 23:25 *Woe unto you, scribes and Pharisees,* ***hypocrites****! for ye make clean the outside of the cup and of the platter, but within they are full of extortion and excess.*

In Rev. 17:5 *(5) And upon her forehead was a name written, Mystery, Babylon The Great. The Mother Of Harlots And Abominations Of The Earth.* These are the “churches” that have martyred Christians *(God’s Elect)* throughout history. There is always a connection between sex and false religion because both are alluring to the wicked hearts of man. This day as I write, countless liberals want to allow their children of only 3 years old, to have gender-affirming surgery *(changing one's natural born sex).* They are also defending pedophilia and the sexualization of children. The Supreme Court has determined that gay *(homosexual)* marriage is accepted. The perversion doesn’t end there due **to the Godless conniving demagogues, Barack Hussein Obama and Joe Biden**. The public schools want to teach “gay rights”, “okay to be gay”, *(CRT)* “Critical Race Theory”, “drag queen story hour" and countless other "woke" perversions to children in elementary school! If someone uses the wrong "pronoun" concerning a person's real born sex *(gender),* he or she can be arrested and charged with sexual harassment just for being truthful. **The educational system is indoctrinating our children. They teach them a sinful Gender Ideology, one that glories in shame, while they boast of their wickedness.** They are teaching in all academia, what is against God and ALL truths. The school system today is **Liberal. They tell students what to think instead of teaching students to think.** They want to rule over you. We are in a Godless "Entitlement" and a "Me" generation. Today, kids are taught and believe they can now change their own sex, by selecting their own gender and have created 72 different Godless "genders". Schools now teach that truth is not absolute; you can choose your own truth and be your own god. They teach "half-truths" which are nothing more than big lies. There is no my truth or your truth, but THE TRUTH. **The Bible is the inspired *(God-***

breathed) **Word of God.** It is the Absolute Truth. There is now even a "Pride Month" to celebrate their perversions! **The truth in any capacity concerning the world is offensive**. Today, using the name **Jesus** is considered harassment! They have taken the word "Boy" out of Boy Scouts to be more inclusive; it's now Scouting America. The world wants to **push a Feminist Agenda, from Satan.** It started with our children; we allowed schools to teach a controlling Godless perverted lifestyle. They are training children to exult and gloat a false narrative. They use evil immoral pride and political correctness, over Biblical Correctness. **Anything contrary to scripture is Godless.** Despite all that, they are still our *"Mission Field"* and they need the Jesus of The Bible. However, there is a point where God gives them up to their own demise. **God destroyed Sodom and Gomorrah as an example of the very things being taught in public schools today!** This moral decay is a Disgrace! **Staying well-informed is vital**. When you don't, you give up on your country, state, city, and neighbor. Many "churches" have accepted gay weddings, as well as offer "blessings" for perversions. **God calls it an Abomination!** Then those who defend it, or condone such will share in God's Judgment of it. Let's visit **James 4:17 ESV** *So whoever knows the right thing to do and fails to do it, for him it is sin.* Also, look at **Proverbs 17:15** *He that justifieth the wicked, and he that condemneth the just, even they both are abomination to the Lord.* ***These are the Birth Pains of The Rapture*** *(Pages 26, 158-163,197-200).* These final perversions of a one-religion "church" will most likely come from Roman Catholics. **They have deeply betrayed true Christianity** and they have the largest following worldwide. Let's look at **Proverbs 3:7 ... *fear the Lord, and depart from evil.***

> **"God's Word supersedes man's law; sin even if legalized by man, is still SIN in the sight of God. His Doctrine is NOT ours to change!"**
>
> Joseph Malara, *Theologian*

In Rev. 17:6 *(6) And I saw the woman drunken with the blood of the saints, and with* *the blood of the martyrs of Jesus: and when I saw her, I wondered with great admiration.* This includes all those who were faithful to Christ and His written Word. They were killed or will be killed because of such loyalty, even those right up to and during The Great Tribulation. They will be rewarded by Jesus. **False religious systems and false churches are responsible for killing millions of God's Chosen People.**

In Rev. 17:7 *(7) And the angel said unto me, Wherefore didst thou marvel? I will tell thee the mystery of the woman, and of the beast that carrieth her, which hath the seven heads and ten horns.* In this verse we see the angel telling the Apostle John not to wonder because he will explain. The **Beast is the *(Antichrist)*,** The **false religious system is the *(Harlot)***. The **seven heads represent seven *(mountains; empires)*** or could mean Rome *(which sits on 7 hills)*. The **ten horns represent ten "kings"** *(temporary leaders)*. Undoubtedly, for a short time, all will be impacted and supported by Satan.

In Rev. 17:8 *(8) The beast that thou sawest was, and is not; and shall ascend out of the bottomless pit, and go into perdition: and they that dwell on the earth shall wonder, whose names were not written in the* ***book of life*** *from the foundation of the world, when they behold the beast that was, and is not, and yet is.* In this verse, we are reminded of the false resurrection of the Beast *(see chapter 13)*. He will be possessed by a demon and many will be fooled into believing that he is God. Those written in the Book of Life ***(God's Elect)*** **are God's Possessions**. This book *(Book of Life)* was written before the foundation of the world. Those written in it will NOT be fooled by the evil Antichrist.

In Rev. 17:9-10 *(9) And here is the mind which hath wisdom. The seven heads are seven mountains, on which the woman sitteth. (10) And there are seven kings: five are fallen, and one is, and the other is not yet come; and when he cometh, he must continue a short space.* In verses 9-10 at this future time there will be seven "kings" or representatives of nations. They will be allowed **a brief time of apparent victory**, then shortly, there's Hell to pay.

In Rev. 17:11-12 *(11) And the beast that was, and is not, even he is the eighth, and is of the seven, and goeth into perdition. (12) And the ten horns which thou sawest are ten kings, which have received no kingdom as yet; but receive power as kings one hour with the beast.* We see The Antichrist is considered both the 7th and 8th kingdom. When we read, *to go into perdition* this explains that Hell shortly awaits him and his time will be short.

In Rev. 17:13-14 *(13) These have one mind, and shall give their power and strength unto the beast. (14) These shall make war with the Lamb, and the Lamb shall overcome them: for he is Lord of Lords and King of kings: and they that are with him are called, and chosen, and faithful.* We see here that all the remaining nations will relinquish their control, influence, and power to The Antichrist. However, here is a look at the end of the ***(War of Armageddon)***. **Jesus, The Lord of Lords will soon destroy all nations and with Him will come His Church, His Elect.**

In Rev. 17:15-16 *(15) And he saith unto me, The waters which thou sawest, where the whore* *sitteth, are peoples, and multitudes, and nations, and tongues. (16) And the ten horns which thou sawest upon the beast, these shall hate the whore, and shall make her desolate and naked, and shall eat her flesh, and burn her with fire.* We see The Antichrist will go against the nations fighting for him, even the apostate church *(One World Region).* This will be to gain all power and false glory and worship for himself. This same **false pride** caused an angel *(Lucifer)* to become the Devil *(Satan).* It is apparent that **PRIDE** is a consistent trend of evil, that will always lead to one's demise. **Power tends to corrupt, and absolute power corrupts absolutely.**

In Rev. 17:17-18 *(17) For God hath put in their hearts to fulfil his will, and to agree, and give their kingdom unto the beast, until the words of God shall be fulfilled. (18) And the woman which thou sawest is that great city, which reigneth over the kings of the earth.* The plan for the nations to relinquish all power over to The Antichrist was all God's doing, His Will. **The *(Great City)* is the place of The Antichrist's empire known as *(Babylon).***

Chapter 18

Commentary *Revelation Chapter 18*

In Rev. 18:1 *(1) And after these things saw another angel come down from heaven, aving great power; and the earth was ightened with his glory.* The term here "After hese things" means, after the series of udgments, *7 seals*, *7 trumpets*, *3 woes*, and *bowls* of wrath. This includes all the Divine atastrophes that will occur. Then the end of he Great Tribulation will be near. There will e a powerful angel from Heaven who will ring light back to the Earth. Remember it as in darkness back in chapter 16 verse 10.

In Rev. 18:2 *(2) And he cried mightily ith a strong voice, saying, Babylon the great fallen, is fallen, and is become the abitation of devils, and the hold of every foul pirit, and a cage of every unclean and ateful bird.* The Angel will proclaim loudly at **Babylon the *(Great City)* has fallen**. othing will be left but wickedness, foul pirits, damage, carnage, and death.

In Rev. 18:3 *(3) For all nations have drunk of the wine of the wrath of her fornication, and the kings of the earth have committed fornication with her, and the merchants of the earth are waxed rich through the abundance of her delicacies.* We read here that all their worship will be for their false *(idols)* gods. Their *(One World Order)* in every capacity has come to this, complete ruin. The kings, unbelieving, false converts, rich and poor have all knowingly committed abominations *(sins)* against God, sexually and in countless other ways.

In Rev. 18:4 *(4) And I heard another voice from heaven, saying, Come out of her, my people, that ye be not partakers of her sins, and that ye receive not of her plagues.* This will be the last call from God, calling out possibly the remnant of His Elect *(My People)*. However, **a depraved heart will not exchange sin for righteousness.** They prefer darkness over light, so their sins are not exposed. **They will be without excuse.**

In Rev. 18:5 *(5) For her sins have reached unto heaven, and God hath remembered her iniquities.* **God will pass Judgment on what's left of *Babylon* and the *Earth*, as a whole.**

In Rev. 18:6-7 *(6) Reward her even as she rewarded you, and double unto her double according to her works: in the cup which she hath filled fill to her double. (7) How much she hath glorified herself, and lived deliciously, so much torment and sorrow give her: for she saith in her heart, I sit a queen, and am no widow, and shall see no sorrow.* This speaks of the Judgment of God. It will be upon all those **who will boast of pride in themselves.** They will have no real sorrow, remorse, or repentance over their sins. They will do the bidding of their daddy, *Satan.*

In Rev. 18:8-9 *(8) Therefore shall her plagues come in one day, death, and mourning, and famine; and she shall be utterly burned with fire: for strong is the Lord God who judgeth her. (9) And the kings of the earth, who have committed fornication and* *lived deliciously with her, shall bewail her, and lament for her, when they shall see the smoke of her burning.* This speaks of God's Judgment, which He will complete in a day. **Those alive will weep for their extreme loss. However, NOT for their extreme SINS against a Holy and Righteous God.**

In Rev. 18:10-11 *(10) Standing afar off for the fear of her torment, saying, Alas, alas that great city Babylon, that mighty city! for in one hour is thy judgment come. (11) And the merchants of the earth shall weep and mourn over her; for no man buyeth their merchandise any more:* We see more of the same. Their self-pity and remorse are for loss, but not for their sins. **Remember all and every single one of our sins are against God Almighty.**

In Rev. 18:12 *(12) The merchandise of gold, and silver, and precious stones, and of pearls, and fine linen, and purple, and silk, and scarlet, and all thyine wood, and all manner vessels of ivory, and all manner vessels of most precious wood, and of brass, and iron, and marble,* This is speaking of their future loss of merchandise because of the great devastation.

In Rev. 18:13 *(13) And cinnamon, and odours, and ointments, and frankincense, and wine, and oil, and fine flour, and wheat, and beasts, and sheep, and horses, and chariots, and slaves, and souls of men.* Their loss included everything; this list explains it all in detail. **The greatest loss will be their souls, thrown into The Lake of Fire, *Hell.***

In Rev. 18:14 *(14) And the fruits that thy soul lusted after are departed from thee, and all things which were dainty and goodly are departed from thee, and thou shalt find them no more at all.* This includes their material desires, goals, and foolish ambitions. **Hence, all earthly possessions.**

In Rev. 18:15 *(15) The merchants of these things, which were made rich by her, shall stand afar off for the fear of her torment, weeping and wailing,* They will continue to speak of their great losses. However, there will be everlasting torment to come.

In Rev. 18:16 *(16) And saying, Alas, alas that great city, that was clothed in fine linen, and purple, and scarlet, and decked with gold, and precious stones, and pearls!* The once "Great City" will be put to ruins.

In Rev. 18:17 *(17) For in one hour so great riches is come to nought. And every shipmaster, and all the company in ships, and sailors, and as many as trade by sea, stood afar off,* The ship owners will be in tears because of **their material losses**.

In Rev. 18:18 *(18) And cried when they saw the smoke of her burning, saying, What city is like unto this great city!* They will seriously mourn over what they will see.

In Rev. 18:19 *(19) And they cast dust on their heads, and cried, weeping and wailing, saying, Alas, alas that great city, wherein were made rich all that had ships in the sea by reason of her costliness! for in one hour is she made desolate*. The dust will be a sign of mourning. That once Great City will be desolate, a wasteland. The above verses are a detailed description of the damage and the personal sorrows. This is all **without crying out to God through Jesus Christ for God's Mercy.** They will worry about shallow, temporal things, but eternal things, not at all. **This is the situation of the whole world today**; they are cavalier concerning eternity. God's Word will not be mocked nor negated because of one's pride or unbelief. **Modern Christianity doesn't want to know the Prince of Peace, they just want to SIN in peace.**

In Rev. 18:20 *(20) Rejoice over her, thou heaven, and ye holy apostles and prophets; for God hath avenged you on her.* This Angel will encourage all *The Tribulation martyrs (which will include the Old Testament Prophets and New Testament Apostles)* that God's Justice has triumphed. God will at that future time avenge them all.

In Rev. 18:21 *(21) And a mighty angel took up a stone like a great millstone, and cast it into the sea, saying, Thus with violence shall that great city Babylon be thrown down, and shall be found no more at all.* A millstone was a large stone of over 100 pounds. This is an allegory that expresses the violence of that once *(Great City)*, which will finally end.

In Rev. 18:22-23 *(22) And the voice of harpers, and musicians, and of pipers, and trumpeters, shall be heard no more at all in thee; and no craftsman, of whatsoever craft he be, shall be found any more in thee; and the sound of a millstone shall be heard no more at all in thee; (23) And the light of a candle shall shine no more at all in thee; and the voice of the bridegroom and of the bride shall be heard no more at all in thee: for thy merchants were the great men of the earth; for by thy sorceries were all nations deceived.* This signifies there will be no more life as once known, no more marriages, no more buying or selling. **Their end is at the doorway for those still alive, worldwide.**

In Rev. 18:24 *(24) And in her was found the blood of prophets, and of saints, and of all that were slain upon the earth.* **God will always avenge the killing of His People. False religious systems like the**

Catholic movement and other cults killed many. True Christians *(Elect)* are hated without a cause but it's actually people's HATE for God, His Word, and His Truths.

Here we see everything concerning God's Perfect Plan coming to fruition. In Roman numeral I *(page 9)* I wrote, Let's suppose YOU love Jesus even a little bit before reading this book. Afterward, you will love Him much more than you ever thought possible. Then again, if YOU don't love Him too much today, by the end of this book YOU will HATE HIM without a cause. Which way are you going? I ask you up to this point in this book, does God display His Love for you? Do you see what is happening as Righteous? There will be Billions and Billions killed, men women, children, and babies. Does that offend you or do you see it as Righteous and rejoice? At this point, do you see your sins as God sees them, hideous? Do YOU love Him more NOW or Hate Him without a cause? Save your answers until the end of this book. My email address is in the beginning pages, feel free to email me personally if you like.

Chapter 19

Commentary *Revelation Chapter 19*

In Rev. 19:1 *(1) And after these things I heard a great voice of much people in heaven, saying, Alleluia; Salvation, and glory, and honour, and power, unto the Lord our God:* **It will be a time for all in Heaven to Praise the Lord.** The Righteous destruction of Babylon *(The Great Whore, Great City)* will end. This will start the next phase of God's Plan as He ends The Great Tribulation. **God's Will, will be utterly and completely accomplished. His enemies will be dealt with. His Elect will be vindicated, and His Sovereignty, Glory, and Justice will reign forever.**

In Rev. 19:2 *(2) For true and righteous are his judgments: for he hath judged the great whore, which did corrupt the earth with her fornication, and hath avenged the blood of his servants at her hand.* This verse moves to interpret the verse before it and includes all Saints. This is one thing I know and **I suspect, that all Believers feel deep inside**

the same way, that we cannot wait for all sin to end. We long for a sinless existence with the Righteousness of God, in an eternity where we can Praise the Lord and bathe in His Glory perpetually.

In Rev. 19:3 *(3) And again they said, Alleluia And her smoke rose up for ever and ever.* This smoke will be from the "One World System", *(Babylon)* including of course the whole world.

In Rev. 19:4 *(4) And the four and twenty elders and the four beasts fell down and worshipped God that sat on the throne, saying, Amen; Alleluia.* In Heaven, all The Church, Elect, and Angels *(creatures)* will fall down in worship. This will be a continuous harmony in Heaven. If you don't love worshipping God *(Jesus)* where you are right now, then Heaven will not be for you.

In Rev. 19:5 *(5) And a voice came out of the throne, saying, Praise our God, all ye his servants, and ye that fear him, both small and great.* This will be a call out to ALL of God's servants *(from whatever rank or level* *both small and great)* to magnify the Lord for all He has done! Hallelujah!

In Rev. 19:6 *(6) And I heard as it were the voice of a great multitude, and as the voice of many waters, and as the voice of mighty thunderings, saying, Alleluia: for the Lord God omnipotent reigneth.* There will be a pinnacle of Praise reaching out far and wide for our Lord. Our praises to God will be of immeasurable power, size, and Glory.

In Rev. 19:7 *(7) Let us be glad and rejoice, and give honour to him: for the <u>marriage of the Lamb is come</u>, and his wife hath made herself ready.* This time will include the Bride *(Church)*, the whole Body of Born Again Believers from *Pentecost* to the *Rapture*, and the Groom *(Jesus)*. His Bride *(Church, Elect)* will be adorned in white, showing purity. These white gowns unlike the ones used once in an earthly wedding will be adorned on His Elect for all eternity. This will represent Jesus's Righteousness in us *(His Elect)*.

In Rev. 19:8 *(8) And to her was granted that she should be arrayed in fine linen, clean and white: for the fine linen is the righteousness of saints.* Fine White Linen…

In Rev. 19:9 *(9) And he saith unto me, Write, Blessed are they which are called unto the marriage supper of the Lamb. And he saith unto me, these are the true sayings of God.* A wedding invitation will be sent out rom Heaven. We know the invitation was not sent to the Bride *(Church),* it will be sent to he Old Testament and Tribulation Saints. ndeed, also to all those Saved before Pentecost, who were not part of the Church.

In Rev. 19:10 *(10) And I fell at his feet o worship him. And he said unto me, See hou do it not: I am thy fellowservant, and of hy brethren that have the testimony of Jesus: worship God: for the testimony of Jesus is the pirit of prophecy.* The Apostle John says he ell at the angel's feet. Then he was nmediately reprimanded by the angel. **An ngel is a fellow servant of God based on reation. God's Elect are servants of God**

based on redemption. Therefore, we will be given a higher position than the angels, once in Heaven.

The Apostle Paul reveals a clear insight concerning angels in Heaven. Let's turn to **1 Corinthians 6:2-3** *(2) Do ye not know that the saints shall judge the world? and if the world shall be judged by you, are ye unworthy to judge the smallest matters?* The Apostle Paul is saying **Believers must judge all things!** This passage also refers to the future time when God's Elect will support Jesus in judging the world during the **Millennial Kingdom**. In verse 3, *(3) Know ye not that we shall judge angels? how much more things that pertain to this life?* We see that the Apostle Paul further explains that we will be judging angels in Heaven. **While on Earth, believers must also judge all things using God's Righteous Standards, not those of this fallen world!** The angel emphasizes to John that it's all about JESUS, both the Old and New Testaments. We are all to worship only God collectively not each other and not angels.

In Rev. 19:11 *(11) And I saw heaven opened, and behold a white horse; and he that sat upon him was called Faithful and True, and in righteousness he doth judge and make war.* Jesus came to Earth as a baby. Then He lived a sinless Righteous life, we could not. He came meek and humble; He healed many and was the Savior to His People. He rose from the dead to prove He was God. He was the Propitiation *(the satisfaction)* for the sins of those His Father chose before the foundation of the world. **His 2nd COMING will be as a Warrior, back to the same sinful, corrupt, and Godless world He left. He will come this time as a LION to destroy, kill, and avenge His Name.** He will take control of the world with His Redeemed and His Angels. He will overthrow all the demons including the Antichrist, The False Prophet, and Satan. He will use His Two-Edged Sword and **His Miraculous Divine Words.**

In Rev. 19:12 *(12) His eyes were as a flame of fire, and on his head were many crowns; and he had a name written, that no* *man knew, but he himself.* This is our Lord of Lords! Oh, what a Glorious Day this will be!

In Rev. 19:13 *(13) And he was clothed with a vesture dipped in blood: and his name is called The Word of God.* Let's visit **John 1:1** ***In the beginning was the Word, and the Word was with God, and the Word was God.***

In Rev. 19:14 *(14) And the armies which were in heaven followed him upon white horses, clothed in fine linen, white and clean.* These are God's Elect, Redeemed *(fine linen)* since angelic beings wouldn't need a horse. Jesus also brings legions and legions of angels to do His bidding.

In Rev. 19:15 *(15) And out of his mouth goeth a sharp sword, that with it he should smite the nations: and he shall rule them with a rod of iron: and he treadeth the winepress of the fierceness and wrath of Almighty God.* We see that all victory will come out of the mouth of Jesus. **His Words are His Sharp Sword. He will rule with a righteous rod of**

iron. There is nothing, nor anyone who can stand in His way to halt or thwart His Plans.

In Rev. 19:16 *(16) And he hath on his vesture and on his thigh a name written, King Of Kings, And Lord Of Lords.* Jesus will wear a robe with a banner along His thigh proclaiming that He is the "King of Kings" and "Lord of Lords". He is The Sovereign God and everyone will submit to His Will.

In Rev. 19:17 *(17) And I saw an angel standing in the sun; and he cried with a loud voice, saying to all the fowls that fly in the midst of heaven, Come and gather yourselves together unto the supper of the great God;* This will be the harsh description of the end of The Great Tribulation, **the results from the War of Armageddon**. The bodies will be lined up and the remains reveal the bloodbath from going against a Holy and Righteous God.

In Rev. 19:18 *(18) That ye may eat the flesh of kings, and the flesh of captains, and the flesh of mighty men, and the flesh of horses, and of them that sit on them, and the* *flesh of all men, both free and bond, both small and great.* This describes the birds *(vultures)* feeding on carrion *(flesh)* which will be the countless dead bodies of those who will be killed. The armies both mighty and powerful, young and old, will be executed by the **Words of God, His Two-Edged Sword.**

In Rev. 19:19 *(19) And I saw the beast, and the kings of the earth, and their armies, gathered together to make war against him that sat on the horse, and against his army.* This is a look at the proposed onslaught of the opposing armies. You should know **going against God in any capacity is futile and suicidal.** The Redeemed will not fight but witness the short and decisive victory.

In Rev. 19:20 *(20) And the beast was taken, and with him the false prophet that wrought miracles before him, with which he deceived them that had received the mark of the beast, and them that worshipped his image. These both were cast alive into a lake of fire burning with brimstone.* These both will be captured and cast alive into **The Lake of**

Fire burning with brimstone. **The Beast *(Antichrist)* and The False Prophet will have the distinction of being the FIRST TWO to be cast into HELL, even before Satan.** They will be equipped with a body that feels the everlasting pain but will never burn up and never be consumed.

In Rev. 19:21 *(21) And the remnant were slain with the sword of him that sat upon the horse, which sword proceeded out of his mouth: and all the fowls were filled with their flesh.* The birds will be filled with their remains. **The Great Tribulation ends.**

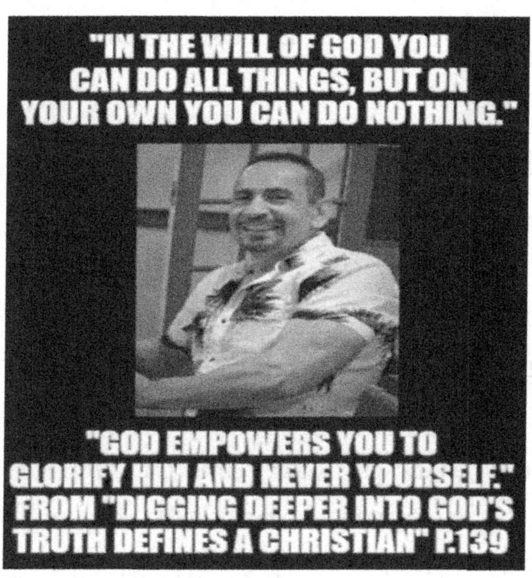

Chapter 20

Commentary *Revelation Chapter 20*

In Rev. 20:1 *(1) And I saw an angel come down from heaven, having the key of the bottomless pit and a great chain in his hand.* **Before the Millennium, Satan will be bound. God will send an angel to bind him.**

In Rev. 20:2 *(2) And he laid hold on the dragon, that old serpent, which is the Devil, and Satan, and bound him a thousand years,* The angel will **capture Satan** and throw him into **The Bottomless Pit**. This is **NOT** Hell *(The Lake of Fire)* but a **temporary holding place.**

In Rev. 20:3 *(3) And cast him into the bottomless pit, and shut him up, and set a seal upon him, that he should deceive the nations no more, till the thousand years should be fulfilled: and after that he must be loosed a little season.* Satan will not be able to use and abuse believers or unbelievers, regarding his power and influence for the next 1000 years. This must be taken factually meaning one thousand literal years.

In Rev. 20:4 *(4) And I saw thrones, and they sat upon them, and judgment was given unto them: and I saw the souls of them that were beheaded for the witness of Jesus, and for the word of God, and which had not worshipped the beast, neither his image, neither had received his mark upon their foreheads, or in their hands; and they lived and reigned with Christ a thousand years.* This speaks of the Tribulation martyrs *(Saints)* who will **not** take the Mark of the Beast. They will live and reign on Earth with Christ and His Elect for 1000 years. Let's turn to **Matthew 24:31 NASB** *And He will send forth His angels with a great trumpet blast, and they will gather together* ***His elect*** *from the four winds, from one end of the sky to the other.* Indeed, God's Elect.

In Rev. 20:5 *(5) But the rest of the dead lived not again until the thousand years were finished. This is the first resurrection.* This is a sobering passage. Those who are unsaved *(not redeemed)* will **not** be removed from **Sheol** or **Hades** *(temporary place of punishment),* until **The Great White Throne Judgment, aka Judgment Day**. This is true for **all** who were **not** saved by God, from the days of Adam and Eve, until ***after*** the 1000-year reign. **There is no one in Hell as of today.** If your "pastor" tells you there are many in Hell today; **find another pastor** *Eschatological Judgments (Pages 274-275).*

In Rev. 20:6 *(6) Blessed and holy is he that hath part in the first resurrection: on such the second death hath no power, but they shall be priests of God and of Christ, and shall reign with him a thousand years.* This is speaking of all those Born Again by God. **The first death is a physical death and the second death is Spiritual.** Those which the second death has no power means, absent with the body, present with the Lord. When a Born Again by God Believer dies, his or her soul enters Heaven immediately. **Again, those who die and are not saved *(unredeemed)* will not leave *Hades* until Judgment Day. Then they will be Judged**

and thrown into the Lake of Fire aka Hell. This is AFTER the Millennium!

<u>What will happen during the 1000-year reign</u>? We know **Satan is bound** in the Bottomless Pit; therefore, his influence is not attacking mankind. We know that The **Antichrist** *(The Beast)* and The **False Prophet** are both **in Hell**. They are at this future time the only ones that will be there. Furthermore, **countless sinners are in *Hades* awaiting Judgment Day.** During this 1000-year reign, the Earth will have no demon or satanic influences. **Jesus Himself** will be our only **King**. His Elect will help rule the Earth through His Righteousness. We must conclude that perhaps those who were among God's pre-elect were spared, possibly their offspring. Consequently, those alive will bear children and the Earth will be repopulated; they will build again. Moreover, **there will be peace and no wars, for 1000 years.** We know we will be **reigning as co-rulers with Christ** during The Millennium. Jesus may **assign His Elect positions** and governing responsibilities worldwide.

Let's look again at **Revelation 2:25-26 LSB** *Nevertheless, what you have, hold fast until I come. And he who overcomes, and he who keeps My deeds until the end, to him* ***I will give authority over the nations;***

Let's turn now to **Matthew 25:20-21** *so he that had received five talents came and brought other five talents, saying, Lord, thou deliveredst unto me five talents: behold, I have gained beside them five talents more. His lord said unto him, Well done, thou good and faithful servant: thou hast been faithful over a few things,* ***I will make thee ruler over many things: enter thou into the joy of thy lord.*** We can also surmise being used by God by looking back at the last part of **Revelation 20:4** ... ***and they lived and reigned with Christ a thousand years.***

Let's turn again to **1 Corinthians 6:2** *Do ye not know that the saints shall judge the world?...* This all indicates God's Elect will help Jesus **Judge** the **Earth** through The Millennium. We know this **is** speaking of the

Millennium **because Christians have little to NO influence in judging the world today.**

In Rev. 20:7 *(7) And when the thousand years are expired, Satan shall be loosed out of his prison.* This would again be a literal 1000 years. The Bible picks up where we left off. Yet, doesn't speak of what will occur during the 1000-year reign, we can only speculate. Then God will allow Satan to come out of his holding place. There are over a hundred and forty verses in the Bible about Hell. However, the lost don't believe it exists. Yet, disbelief will not negate its existence.

In Rev. 20:8 *(8) And shall go out to deceive the nations which are in the four quarters of the earth, Gog, and Magog, to gather them together to battle: the number of whom is as the sand of the sea.* **Then Satan, once set free will go right back to deceiving the world.** He will set out to bring a unified evil, a war of **rebellion against Jerusalem**. Satan will convince nations around the world to gather one last time.

This comes after the 1000-year reign. **This shows how easily man can be deceived by Satan. This reminds me of today's "Fake News".** It is and has been controlling, manipulating, deceiving, and feeding the Godless liberal mind propaganda and even paid propaganda for many decades. This speaks to man as being evil with a wicked depraved heart. **We are all born with a heart deceitful above all things but for the Grace of God**.

In Rev. 20:9 *(9) And they went up on the breadth of the earth, and compassed the camp of the saints about, and the beloved city: and fire came down from God out of heaven, and devoured them*. **God will not tolerate for one minute, any more nonsense! He will promptly use Divine Judgment and kill them all!**

In Rev. 20:10 *(10) And the devil that deceived them was cast into the lake of fire and brimstone, where the beast and the false prophet are, and shall be tormented day and night for ever and ever.* Now, do you remember Revelation 19:20? The first two inhabitants of **"The Lake of Fire"**, will be *The Beast* and *The False Prophet.* When this time comes Satan will be there as well. **This will be his final everlasting Judgment. This will also be the final destination of ALL the lost, *(non-elect)* unredeemed.**

In Rev. 20:11 *(11) And I saw a great white throne, and him that sat on it, from whose face the earth and the heaven fled away; and there was found no place for them.* **The Great White Throne is where Jesus will pass judgment on the *(lost)* unredeemed.** Jesus tells us in **Matthew 24:35** *Heaven and earth shall pass away, but my words shall not pass away.* In **2 Peter 3:10** *But the day of the Lord will come as a thief in the night; in the which the heavens shall pass away with a great noise, and the elements shall melt with fervent heat, the earth also and the works that are therein shall be burned up*. This speaks of **His 2nd Coming**. **He will come as a thief in the night.** Then it speaks of our future. Then moves to speak of God burning up the Earth.

In Rev. 20:12 *(12) And I saw the dead, small and great, stand before God; and the books were opened: and another book was opened, which is the book of life: and the dead were judged out of those things which were written in the books, according to their works.* This is to say that there are undoubtedly degrees of punishment, that will depend on the actions *(works)* of each one's life. **At that time, all of God's Redeemed *(Elect)* will be in Heaven. They will NOT WITNESS THIS and are not included in this Judgment.** Again, those whose names are written in the **Book of Life** are excluded from this.

In Rev. 20:13 *(13) And the sea gave up the dead which were in it; and death and hell delivered up the dead which were in them: and they were judged every man according to their works.* **This verse means all who died at sea from the flood of Noah's day and otherwise since the beginning of time will be there.** Where it says "death and hell"; the word Hell here means ***(Hades)*** a holding place for the unredeemed. Then there are other times when the word *Sheol* is used. Again, there is no one in Hell until a 1000 years after the Antichrist and his sidekick the False Prophet are thrown there. Remember, they will be the first two in **Hell.** This is many, many years from now; after the Millennial *(1000-year)* Reign.

Let's look at **Matthew 25:32-34 LSB** *(32) And all the nations will be gathered before Him; and He will separate them from one another, as the shepherd separates the sheep from the goats; (33) and He will put the* ***sheep on His right****, and the* ***goats on the left****. (34) "Then the King will say to those on His right, 'Come, you who are blessed of My Father, inherit the kingdom, which has been prepared for you from the foundation of the world.* This paints a clear picture…God can never make a mistake…

"A time will come when instead of SHEPHERDS feeding the SHEEP, the Church will have CLOWNS ENTERTAINING the GOATS."

Charles H. Spurgeon, *Prince of Pastors*

In Rev. 20:14 LSB *14) Then death and Hades were thrown into the lake of fire. This is the second death.* I am using the **LSB** *(Legacy Standard Bible)*, which correctly says Hades. Again, throughout most of this book unless specified I have used the **KJV** *(King James Version)* Bible. This passage explains that ALL who stand before Jesus on **Judgment Day** will have NO defense for their sins. **They will ALL be found knowingly guilty of SIN. Then all will be thrown into Hell *(everlasting torment)* aka Lake of Fire.**

In Rev. 20:15 *(15) And whosoever was not found written in the book of life was cast into the lake of fire.* This verse stands true for every person ever born. **The Book of Life** was written **before** the foundation of the world. Let's turn to **Ephesians 1:4** *According as he hath chosen us in him before the foundation of the world, that we should be holy and without blame before him in love:* This verse and countless others **takes Salvation out of our hands.** Salvation is always 100% GOD and 0% man.

We must all clearly understand God's Word concerning *Election, Politics* & *Religion.* Also, why *Tithing* is NOT for today and why Christians MUST Judge, and *Judge all things* Righteously. In addition, how to spot *False Teachers.* Please read ***"Digging Deeper into God's Truths Defines a Christian"***

Online Everywhere even Amazon!

"It's not an Option to Exercise Discernment as a Christian, it is a Mandate, it is a Duty."

Justin Peters, *Evangelist, Bible Teacher*

"Where God intends to Regenerate a person, that person is Regenerated and cannot resist God's Will in the matter."

John Owen, *Pastor, Theologian*

Chapter 21

Commentary *Revelation Chapter 21*

In Rev. 21:1 *(1) And I saw a new heaven and a new earth: for the first heaven and the first earth were passed away; and there was no more sea.* The Apostle John sees all this as a witness, **the New Earth and The New Heaven**. God will entirely burn this Earth down, annihilate it, and completely rebuild it. When you hear or meet any ridiculous **"climate change"** activists, try explaining to them that this world is controlled by God alone. He will burn it all down personally. **It will not end by man's doings but by God's Promise. It will end by Divine Judgment, not by a man-made HOAX called climate change!**

Furthermore, the New Earth will not have a sea. The Earth is currently three-fourths water. Therefore, the land will be plentiful without the oceans *(seas)*. There will be only land and no fish. We will all have *Glorified Bodies*. We will be able to do things we cannot yet comprehend e.g. walk through walls and live forever. **Before God does all this, He will have already placed EVERY sinner young and old *(unredeemed)* in Hell, including Satan and all demons.**

In Rev. 21:2 *(2) And I John saw the holy city, new Jerusalem, coming down from God out of heaven, prepared as a bride adorned for her husband* This depicts the **Holy City of Jerusalem** *(dwelling place of God)* aka a *New and better Eden* that will come **down to The New Earth.** This verse encompasses all of the Saints *(Redeemed)* clothed in fine linen. We will all be coming down to the **New Earth and The New Jerusalem.** The Old Earth will be entirely, eradicated. The New Earth will be completely renovated. We will be as prepared as a Bride *(Believers)* adorned for our Groom *(Jesus)* The King of Kings! This is Spiritual…

In Rev. 21:3 *(3) And I heard a great voice out of heaven saying, Behold, the tabernacle of God is with men, and he will dwell with them, and they shall be his people, and God himself shall be with them, and be* *their God.* Here we read that a voice from Heaven *(God),* is declaring that the Tabernacle *(Home)* of God *(Holy City of Jerusalem in Heaven)* will come down. Jesus will live with us and we will be His, Amen!

In Rev. 21:4 *(4) And God shall wipe away all tears from their eyes; and there shall be no more death, neither sorrow, nor crying, neither shall there be any more pain: for the former things are passed away.* This verse should come as a huge sigh of relief to all. The former things will have passed away! **There will be no more sin or death; we will live for eternity with glorified bodies.** We will live our new lives **In Christ**. He will wipe away all of our past tears, sorrows, pains, and our sinful nature as well. He alone is worthy; we will live in total wonder of Him.

Let's turn to **Jeremiah 30:7** *Alas! for that day is great, so that none is like it: it is even the time of Jacob's Trouble, but he shall be saved out of it.* Here we see **Jacob's Trouble**. He was given an insight from God through Jeremiah concerning The

Tribulation. **This vision included the 2nd Coming of Jesus to save Israel** and Jacob was part of God's Salvational Plan! Let's understand who Jacob was, see **Romans 9:13** *As it is written,* ***Jacob*** *have I loved, but Esau have I hated.* God never forgets the Ones who are His, those He loves, His Elect.

In Rev. 21:5 *(5) And he that sat upon the throne said, Behold, I make all things new. And he said unto me, Write: for these words are true and faithful.* We see God *(The Father)* telling The Apostle John to write. These words do ring out to all Believers that God is nothing but the TRUTH. He is Holy, Faithful, True and more than we can ever comprehend.

In Rev. 21:6 *(6) And he said unto me, It is done. I am Alpha and Omega, the beginning and the end. I will give unto him that is athirst of the fountain of the water of life freely.* This verse identifies the speaker as Jesus; **It is done!** He will complete everything He set out to do and **Save everyone His Father gave Him**. He is the Alpha *(the beginning)* and

Omega *(the end)*. Let's read what Jesus tells the multitudes in **Matthew 5:6.** *Blessed are they which do hunger and thirst after righteousness: for they shall be filled*. All those Born Again by God hunger for justice. **We love to expose the evil in this world,** and then exult the name of Jesus above all names. **In Heaven all Believers will gratefully rejoice in Him knowing none are worthy, but Him.**

In Rev. 21:7 *(7) He that* ***overcometh*** *shall inherit all things; and I will be his God, and he shall be my son.* Let's look at **1 John 5:4-5** *(4) For whatsoever is born of God* ***overcometh*** *the world: and this is the victory that* ***overcometh*** *the world, even our faith. (5) Who is he that* ***overcometh*** *the world, but he that believeth that Jesus is the Son of God?* We see that all Believers inherit all things in Heaven. We will have a Heavenly Family and a God that loves us, eternally. **Overcome**...

In Rev. 21:8 *(8) But the fearful, and unbelieving, and the abominable, and murderers, and whoremongers, and* *sorcerers, and idolaters,* ***and all liars****, shall have their part in the lake which burneth with fire and brimstone: which is the second death.* Wholeheartedly, I hope this verse is a solemn warning to you, it has been to many including me. If you don't abandon the wrong course or you see yourself in this verse; it's time to look again, the consequences are also in this same verse. You should know that **True** Christians **live in an unbelieving world, and are in a word, HATED**. Bring it! Here God capsizes a list of dreadful sins, proclaiming those who will NOT be in Heaven. This is a glance at the reality of us all at one time before we were saved and haven't yet gone through a daily process of **Sanctification** *(Spiritual Growth)*. God's Word completely and radically changes our outlook on life and sin. It washes our minds clean and gives us new affections. When one is Truly Born Again by God, he or she is a new creation; old things pass away and behold all things become new. **This is NOT Poetry, but God's Holy Spirit of Truth in action.**

In the life of a true convert, there will always be unmistakable evidence of a transformed life. **There won't be perfection in life, but a New Direction in life.** Let's turn to **1 Corinthians 6:9-11** *(9) Know ye not that the unrighteous shall not inherit the kingdom of God? Be not deceived: neither fornicators, nor idolaters, nor adulterers, nor effeminate, nor abusers of themselves with mankind, (10) Nor thieves, nor covetous, nor drunkards, nor revilers, nor extortioners, shall inherit the kingdom of God. (11) And* ***such were some of you****: but ye are washed, but ye are sanctified, but ye are justified in the name of the Lord Jesus, and* ***by the Spirit of our God.*** **All the good in me is HIM, everything else is my fault.** Christians fall, but when one does, they get back up immediately and run to Jesus.

In Rev. 21:9 *(9) And there came unto me one of the seven angels which had the seven vials full of the seven last plagues, and talked with me saying, Come hither, I will shew thee the bride the Lamb's wife.* This is an angel revealing a Devine Gift of Love **from God The Father to God The Son,** ***His Bride (The Church).*** Thi concerns the splendor of the inheritance His Redeemed *(Elect)* will enjoy for eternity.

In Rev. 21:10 *(10) And he carried me away in the spirit to a great and high mountain, and shewed me that great city, the holy Jerusalem, descending out of heaven from God.* The angel will carry John to a high vantage point, there the Apostle John will see **The New Holy City of Jerusalem.** This will be the center of all things, the dwelling place of Jesus.

In Rev. 21:11 *(11) Having the glory of God: and her light was like unto a stone most precious, even like a jasper stone, clear as crystal;* The Apostle's attempt to place the look of such a glorious place in mere words is not fully conceivable or comprehensible!

In Rev. 21:12 *(12) And had a wall great and high, and had twelve gates, and at the gates twelve angels, and names written thereon, which are the names of the twelve tribes of the children of Israel:* **This reveals walls** of wonder, privacy, care and an overwhelming privilege. The twelve gates will each be guarded by an angel. Furthermore, each **gate** will adorn the names of each of the **Twelve Tribes**. They are the sons of Jacob *(Israel),* which are Reuben, Simeon, Levi, Judah, Issachar, Zebulun, Dan, Naphtali, Gad, Asher, Joseph, and Benjamin.

In Rev. 21:13-14 *(13) On the east three gates; on the north three gates; on the south three gates; and on the west three gates. (14) And the wall of the city had twelve foundations, and in them the names of the twelve apostles of the Lamb.* There will be twelve gates, three on each side: North, South, East, and West. In the center, no doubt will be God and His Holy City, The New Jerusalem. Here we read, that the **foundation** of each wall will display the names of the **Twelve Apostles**; they are *(Simon)* Peter, Andrew, James, John, Phillip, Bartholomew, Thomas, Matthew, Judas *(Thaddaeus),* Simon *(the Zealot),* James, and Paul. When Matthias was chosen by the remaining eleven Apostles in ***Acts 1:26*** it was **before** the Apostles were given the Holy Spirit in the upper room. Therefore, I do believe that The **Apostle Paul did take the place of Judas *(Iscariot).*** The name *Matthias* was never mentioned again in scripture but the Apostle Paul sure was. **The Apostle Paul wrote about**

2/3 of the New Testament books through the Divine influence of The Holy Spirit.

In Rev. 21:15 *(15) And he that talked with me had a golden reed to measure the city, and the gates thereof, and the wall thereof.* Back then, a reed would be roughly ten feet long.

In Rev. 21:16 *(16) And the city lieth foursquare, and the length is as large as the breadth: and he measured the city with the reed, twelve thousand furlongs. The length and the breadth and the height of it are equal.* This City will measure approximately **two million square miles** or roughly 1500 miles cubed, which is larger than the moon!

In Rev. 21:17 *(17) And he measured the wall thereof, an hundred and forty and four cubits, according to the measure of a man, that is, of the angel.* This measurement comes to 216 feet of the thickness *(width)* of the walls! Perhaps, our Glorified *(Spiritual)* Bodies will NOT be able to penetrate it *(go through it)* as Jesus went through the walls *(door)* in the upper room, where His Disciples were *(John 20:19).* He also came out of a closed tomb *(Matthew 28:2).* We will have a body like Christ *(Philippians 3:21).* This may account for the 12 gates *(doorways)* guarded on each side *(Rev. 21:12).* Therefore, no one will go through the *walls* to enter, all must use one of the 12 gates.

In Rev. 21:18 *(18) And the building of the wall of it was of jasper: and the city was pure gold, like unto clear glass*. **The City will be most overwhelming, glamorous, and glorious. The light of glory will come from the radiance of Father God and The King of Kings.** Their light will be piercing through the walls and streets of seemingly pure and clear Gold. **What a wondrous sight that will be! Amen!**

In Rev. 21:19 *(19) And the foundations of the wall of the city were garnished with all manner of precious stones. The first foundation was jasper; the second, sapphire; the third, a chalcedony; the fourth, an emerald;* John is trying to describe a fascinating and miraculous site!

> ***As it is written, There is none righteous, no, not one: There is none that understandeth, there is none that seeketh after God.*** Romans 3:10-11

In Rev. 21:20 *(20) The fifth, sardonyx; the sixth, sardius; the seventh, chrysolyte; the eighth, beryl; the ninth, a topaz; the tenth, a chrysoprasus; the eleventh, a jacinth; the twelfth, an amethyst.* If you look up each stone, some of the names have changed, it is too amazing for mere words to describe!

In Rev. 21:21 *(21) And the twelve gates were twelve pearls: every several gate was of one pearl: and the street of the city was pure gold, as it were transparent glass.* Wow, to think that each gate is one huge pearl is mind-blowing! The streets will be of transparent refined gold, astounding!

In Rev. 21:22 *(22) And I saw no temple therein: for the Lord God Almighty and the Lamb are the temple of it.* **There will no longer be a Temple because Father God and Jesus will be our Temple everlasting.**

In Rev. 21:23 *(23) And the city had no need of the sun, neither of the moon, to shine in it: for the glory of God did lighten it, and the Lamb is the light thereof.* **There will be no night, no dimming of light, no moon, and**

no sun. All our light will be generated and radiated from God and The King of Kings; oh, what a God we serve!

In Rev. 21:24 *(24) And the nations of them which are saved shall walk in the light of it: and the kings of the earth do bring their glory and honour into it.* What a wonderous sight it will be; the people, God's *(Elect)* of all nations will live together in love and peace for all eternity with God Himself.

In Rev. 21:25 *(25) And the gates of it shall not be shut at all by day: for there shall be no night there.* There will be full access for God's Elect in and out of the gates, as they will not be closed.

In Rev. 21:26 *(26) And they shall bring the glory and honour of the nations into it.* All different peoples of the world, every tongue, and every nation will be there. I believe we will all speak the same language in Heaven *(possibly Hebrew).*

In Rev. 21:27 *(27) And there shall in no wise enter into it any thing that defileth,* *neither whatsoever worketh abomination, or maketh a lie: but they which are written in the Lamb's book of life.* This is a reminder to us here and now that the residents of Heaven will only be those Born Again by God, aka those written in the **Book of Life**.

Do you have questions about "Spiritual Gifts" and why and when they ended? Do you want to understand why Catholics are not Christians? Why there aren't any more Prophets or Apostles today? Do you want to increase your knowledge of Biblical jargon, so you won't be bamboozled by others, like I once was? Get a copy, online everywhere, the 7th published book God has allowed me to write. ***"IT'S ALL SUBJECT TO GOD'S WORD" See, www.josephmalara.com***

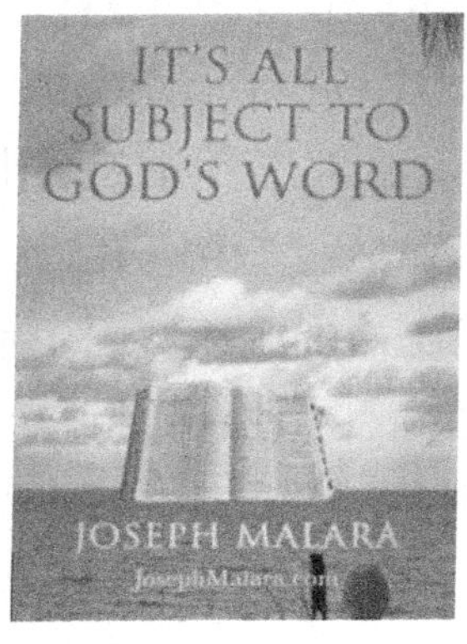

Chapter 22

Commentary *Revelation Chapter 22*

In Rev. 22:1-2 *(1) And he shewed me a pure river of water of life, clear as crystal, proceeding out of the throne of God and of the Lamb.* This is symbolic to say our sustainer will be God. He will be our life, our Joy and our water of life. There will be no thirst because Jesus is our water of life. In verse *(2) In the midst of the street of it, and on either side of the river, was there the tree of life, which bare twelve manner of fruits, and yielded her fruit every month: and the leaves of the tree were for the healing of the nations.* We know sin drove man from the Garden. Yet, Grace will bring man to an eternal Paradise. There could be *rivers* of some sort. The **Tree of Life** will be available to us and we can eat freely from it. There will be twelve different fruits growing on it, perhaps a different fruit periodically or all at the same time. The healing of the nations is more like a maintaining of all our lives, this too is and will be from our Lord, continually.

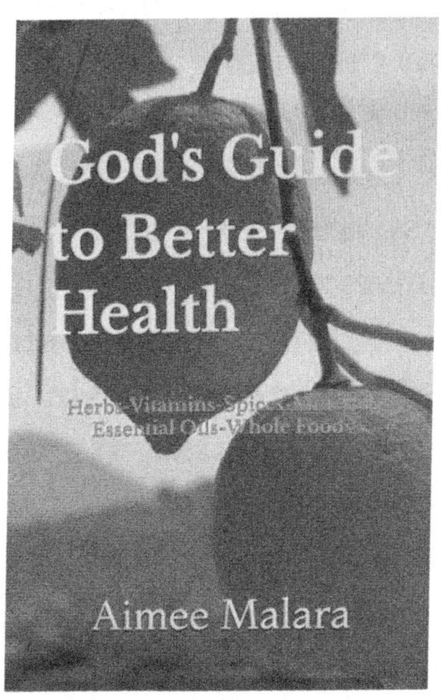

There will be no sickness or ill health in Heaven. However, today as I speak there is ill health. There are **healing oils and foods** from many trees and plants, which were used Biblically. My wife Aimee has written a book that includes the correct uses of many essential oils and whole foods. Get a copy! ***"GOD'S GUIDE TO BETTER HEALTH"*** *is* found online everywhere books are sold, even on Amazon or **www.josephmalara.com** with video info!

In Rev. 22:3 *(3) And there shall be no more curse: but the throne of God and of the Lamb shall be in it; and his servants shall serve him:* The penalty *(curse)* of Adam's sin is *(was)* transferred to everyone through conception. However, this was annulled *(for God's Elect)* at the cross with the shedding of Jesus' blood. **In Genesis 3, sin made its arrival and here it makes its departure.** There will be no need for any more atonements and sacrifices. There will be no need for Jesus to die again. God's Elect will all live in a **sinless** existence and worship our Lord for all eternity.

In Rev. 22:4 *(4) And they shall see his face; and his name shall be in their foreheads.* We will be in our glorified bodies and be able to look at the Face of God both Son and Father. **We will be their possession and marked as such.**

In Rev. 22:5 *(5) And there shall be no night there; and they need no candle, neither light of the sun; for the Lord God giveth them light: and they shall reign for ever and ever.*

We are again reminded of His Wonderful Light and that we will reign in some capacity through Him. We will be regarded over the angels and possibly have certain jobs and responsibilities under God's Provisions.

In Rev. 22:6 *(6) And he said unto me, These sayings are faithful and true: and the Lord God of the holy prophets sent his angel to shew unto his servants the things which must shortly be done.* This confirms that all The Apostle John has witnessed **will come to pass, just as it is written** in both the Old and New Testaments.

In Rev. 22:7 *(7) Behold, I come quickly: blessed is he that keepeth the sayings of the prophecy of this book.* This is reiterated in **Revelation 1:3** *Blessed is he that readeth, and they that hear the words of this prophecy, and keep those things which are written therein: for the time is at hand.* I know rsthand that the constant study of **The Book of Revelation has brought me much, much closer to God and His Truths.** This s our ultimate blessing as Believers. We must keep the things written here in His Word, in our hearts, and then apply them to our everyday lives. It is a huge blessing to be able *(God Willing)* to have many read what this book is **all about, HIM, The Revelation of Jesus Christ, The Lord of Lords.**

In Rev. 22:8 *(8) And I John saw these things, and heard them. And when I had heard and seen, I fell down to worship before the feet of the angel which shewed me these things.* The Apostle John will be utterly overwhelmed, and rightfully so! This also happened before *(see Revelation 19:10).*

In Rev. 22:9 *(9) Then saith he unto me, See thou do it not: for I am thy fellowservant, and of thy brethren the prophets, and of them which keep the sayings of this book: worship God.* Then John will again be reprimanded so that he may understand; that **we serve and worship ONLY God and bow only to Him.** This will come as a big surprise to the apostate Catholic movement that falsely worships Mary.

In Rev. 22:10 *(10) And he saith unto me, Seal not the sayings of the prophecy of this book: for the time is at hand.* This verse is to say, get **The Revelation of Jesus Christ** out to the seven churches *(referred to in chapters 1-3)*, then ultimately out to the world, **this has all been accomplished**.

In Rev. 22:11 *(11) He that is unjust, let him be unjust still: and he which is filthy, let him be filthy still: and he that is righteous, let him be righteous still: and he that is holy, let him be holy still.* **This verse is to say, you reap what you have sown.** Those who say they want nothing to do with God or even politics *(concerning their nation)* are the same ones who remain unjust. They will become noticeably more and more filthy. However, those who grow to love the Lord and every facet of His Word will move closer to Jesus in all Truth. They will be His and be called righteous *(Holy; set aside for Him)*.

In Rev. 22:12 *(12) And, behold, I come quickly; and my reward is with me, to give every man according as his work shall be.*

This is a serious warning to God's Elect. **We must be ready, in the sense that we are caught joyfully doing His bidding, in eager anticipation of His Return. We must run our race as to WIN; BOX as to not hit the air alone.** Certainly, there are times when our "works" may seem worthless, and futile. However, the seeds we regularly plant are seriously examined by God. He is in full control; we must simply be obedient. There will be rewards for those faithful to His Commands. This is regardless of the outcome of our sincere efforts. Moreover, we must **represent Him in all Truth**. This includes and is not limited to social, political, and academic areas. Christians must call out **right** from **wrong** whenever we see it. We must be an example of this world's morality and justice. **There are NO others qualified!**

Let's turn to **1 Corinthians 9:24-26 LSB** *(24) Do you not know that those who run in a race all run, but only one receives the prize? <u>Run in such a way that you may win</u>. (25) Now everyone who competes in the games <u>exercises self-control</u> in all things.*

They then do it to receive a corruptible crown, but we an incorruptible. (26) Therefore I run in such a way, as not without aim; I ***box*** *in such a way, as not beating the air;* Let's also turn to **James 2:18 LSB** *But someone will say, "You have faith; and I have works. Show me your faith without the works, and I will show you my faith by my works."* This verse also speaks volumes. **We must run to win; DO NOT be cavalier about your Salvation!**

In Rev. 22:13 *(13) I am Alpha and Omega, the beginning and the end, the first and the last.* Here we read the words of Jesus which He proclaimed in chapter one. **He again declares this Truth here in the last chapter of the Bible.**

In Rev. 22:14 (*14) Blessed are they that do his commandments, that they may have right to the tree of life, and may enter in through the gates into the city.* This verse does not speak of works to gain Heaven. We know only His Elect will see Heaven. Furthermore, **good works are the fruit (*evidence)* of true Salvation, not the cause**.

For this reason, we must know what His Commandments are **by living in His Word daily. Seriously...**

A better rendering of the translation of this verse is found in **Revelation 22:14 LSB** *Blessed are those who wash their robes, so that they may have the authority to the tree of life and may enter by the gates into the city.* This means all those who have had their sins washed away by the blood of the Lamb *(Jesus)*; **they will be able to eat freely from The Tree of Life.**

In Rev. 22:15 *(15) For without are dogs, and sorcerers, and whoremongers, and murderers, and idolaters, and whosoever loveth and maketh a lie.* These categories identify those of **no moral fiber, liars, murderers, cheaters**, LGBTQ+ (lesbian, gay, bisexual, transgender, queer, and/or questioning), **these abominations are despicable to God. There will be no such people in Heaven.**

Turn to **Hebrews 10:31** ***It is a fearful thing to fall into the hands of the living***

***God.* This should smack each of us in the face! It should terrify us all, producing in us a contrite heart and a Holy Fear of reverence, drawing us closer to Him in Spirit and TRUTH.**

Let's look at **1 Corinthians 6:9-10** *(9) Know ye not that the unrighteous shall not inherit the kingdom of God? Be not deceived: neither fornicators* {the sexually immoral}, *nor idolaters, nor adulterers, nor effeminate* {homosexuals, crossdressers, transvestites}, *nor abusers* {sodomites, men with men} *of themselves with mankind, (10) Nor thieves, nor covetous, nor drunkards, nor revilers, nor extortioners, shall inherit the kingdom of God.* **These verses speak volumes...**

Now turn to **Matthew 10:28** ***And fear not them which kill the body, but are not able to kill the soul: but rather fear <u>HIM</u> which is able to destroy both soul and body in hell.*** This is self-explanatory.

In Rev. 22:16 *(16) I Jesus have sent mine angel to testify unto you these things in the churches. I am the root and the offspring* *of David, and the bright and morning star.* Jesus is the offspring *(physically)* of David *(however still David's Creator)* as foretold by the Prophets. Jesus is The One that will be The Light of The New Day, The Morning Star.

In Rev. 22:17 *(17) And the Spirit and the bride say, Come. And let him that heareth say, Come. And let him that is athirst come. And whosoever will, let him take the water of life freely.* This proclamation is to say all those whom The Holy Spirit has converted are to come. **The Father Chooses us, The Son Redeems us, and The Holy Spirit Seals us.** We should embrace them equally in our affections. We are to come without restrictions and drink up God's Mercy and Grace. Today, His Word is our Fountain of Life. **We must read, search, study, meditate, and drink up His Word, like a thirsty man probing the desert for water!**

There will be a time, ***(Judgment Seat of Christ, aka Bema Seat)*** when Jesus will reward His Own **concerning all of His *(Saints, Elect)*,** who committed unselfish acts and those who lived for the Glory of God in faithful service to Him. Let's look at **2 Corinthians 5:10** *For we must* ***all*** *appear before the judgment seat of Christ; that every one may receive the things done in his body, according to that he hath done, whether it be good or bad.* We read in **Revelation 3:11** *Behold, I come quickly: hold that fast which thou hast, that no man take thy crown.* **Jesus will Judge each of His Elect,** this judgment is not for or connected to one's Salvation. **It will be regarding each Saint's performance, actions, efforts, works, and service to Christ.**

I always tell people we *(Believers)* are not saved by our good works, but saved to do good works! We are commanded by God to tell others of His Gospel, to spread His Good News, and to be a living example of Jesus. **We should know His Word and defend it with PASSION and** have a deep burden praying *(with action)* for lost souls. **If you have no desire to see your family, friends, and neighbors Saved by God, The Holy Spirit is NOT in you.**

In Rev. 22:18 *(18) For I testify unto every man that heareth the words of the prophecy of this book, If any man shall add unto these things, God shall add unto him the plagues that are written in this book:* This verse means don't say what God didn't imply. **In short, don't create a false "jesus", one of your own imagination,** this today seems to be the norm *(Pages 22-24)*. There are few who use the correct **Hermeneutics,** which is suitable for the interpretation of scripture. We must use the correct interpretational standards concerning **Exegesis** and **Eisegesis**. Standing your ground, In Truth...

In Rev. 22:19 *(19) And if any man shall take away from the words of the book of this prophecy, God shall take away his part out of the book of life, and out of the holy city, and from the things which are written in this book.* **This warning refers to the whole Bible of 66 books.** There can be no more severe warning from God towards His Elect. This is why I feel very compelled to study, that I may be correct and NOT misinterpreting His Holy Word. I will stop now and pray...

Quoting, Charles Spurgeon, ***"There is a BIG difference in being right, and almost right."***

In Rev. 22:20 *(20) He which testifieth these things saith, Surely I come quickly. Amen. Even so, come, Lord Jesus.* Jesus said when He comes **it will be quick, not soon**. It has been about two thousand years since the time of these Holy Writings. What I do see today is that it is all lining up. God allows Satan to do what's needed to bring the Glorifying End we have just read. His timing is not our timing. **We are NOT looking for any more "signs" we are looking up for His return, Rapture.** The **blessed hope** is not that The Tribulation is coming, but Christ. **Be ready, and keep looking up, the Best is yet to come.** The Pharisees could not recognize Jesus who was right before their eyes as the true Messiah. In the same way today, many cannot recognize the signs of The Rapture, right before their eyes. The ***birth pains*** **of the Rapture** are with us daily *(Pages 26, 158-163, 197-200).*

In Rev. 22:21 *(21) The grace of our Lord Jesus Christ be with you all. Amen.* Some Bible interpretations *(versions)* use the word *(Saints)* in place of *all.* This benediction of His Grace is also my prayer to all who read this book, I say this, not because my book is special but because **His Word** is. **He said all who read The Book of Revelation will be blessed,** once you have come to this page you have completely read the whole book of Revelation. **Be Blessed...** Undoubtedly, everything God said will come to pass; you can bet your life on it...

Do YOU need ***"straight talk"*** as YOU search for, or deal with a real **Christian Relationship? "The Guide to Christian Dating, Marriage and Sex"** Now on Amazon!

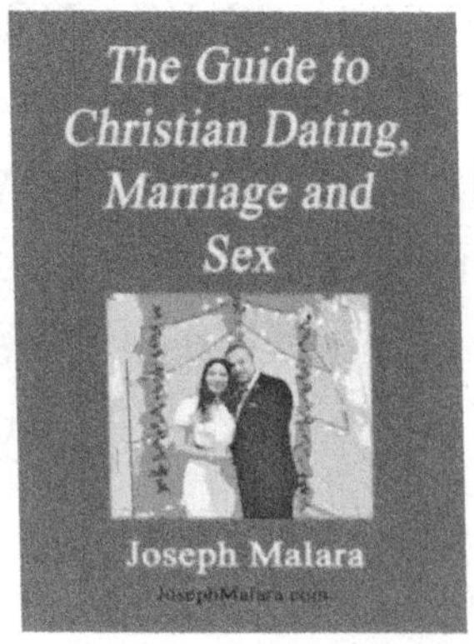

Beware of Creating a "god" of YOUR OWN Making!

- All Accepting, No Rejecting
- All LOVE, No HATE
- All YOU, Not Him *(Jesus)*
- All Grace, No Judgment
- All Mercy, No WRATH
- All Forgiveness, No Repentance
- All Heaven, NO HELL
- All Your way, No SIN
- All Pride, No Humility
- All Unbiblical, No TRUTH

This is NOT the GOD of Scripture!

For what shall it profit a man, if he shall gain the whole world, and lose his own soul? Mark 8:36

Chapter 23

(Types of Beliefs) The following is a short list of words used to describe certain **avenues of end-time beliefs.**

• **Preterism** - a Preterist doesn't believe in a Millennium, they believe it has already taken place *(unbiblical).*

• **Futurists** – they interpret The Book of Revelation in a literal manner as one should. They understand some passages are of course symbolic *(Biblical).*

• **Idealism** – they see and interpret the Book of Revelation as symbolic. They don't see a need for God *(unbiblical).*

• **Historical** – a simple wide view of Christianity from a historical aspect. However, The Book of Revelation is prophetic *(Biblical).*

• **Dispensationalism** - is simply a term meaning a title for theology that recognizes a system God *uses* to divide history or ages as "dispensations". This system originated in the mid-1900s. However, we should interpret scripture on its merit alone. There is a difference between the Church and Israel. This system has many different distinctions, some Biblical and others not.

- **Non-dispensational** – has no place for Israel in the future. They spiritualize everything in the Bible and nothing is literal *(unbiblical)*.

- **Covenant Theology** – they would spiritualize the Bible rather than interpret it accurately. It's an explanatory framework to overview the structure of scripture. Some of their views are Biblical some are not.

- **Amillennialism** – the letter *A* used before a word means against. They do not believe in the Millennium; *this view started in the late 1800's*. They state that the 1000-year reign is merely symbolic *(figurative)* and NOT literal. This is to say they disagree with scripture when it clearly says one thousand years, which is repeated six times in chapter 20. They state that when Jesus returns to Earth after The Great Tribulation, that's

Judgment Day, however, biblically it's not, it's **The 2nd Coming.** They reject the Rapture and in some ways are *pessimistic.* They believe the Millennium started in the New Testament and is ongoing, as I write. They believe that the Church is reigning now. We know that is not true; by holding to this view, one would have to discount that when God says Israel, He means the Church. There is no exegetical basis for this Biblical view. However, some of the views they believe are true, and some are not.

- **Postmillennialism** - they take an *optimistic* belief that the second coming of Jesus comes after the Millennium. They see the 1000 years as bringing great prosperity to the Church. They say Christ will come after "Christians" make the world better. We can undoubtedly see that the world is getting worse each day. The Christian faith is threatened more with each passing day. We can see that corruption, apostasy, and worldwide evil increases daily. They reject the Rapture. They believe the Church is Israel *(unbiblical).*

• **Premillennialism** – Pre-tribulation, is a Biblical view. This states that God will return in the air, *The Rapture* before the Tribulation starts. This understanding as you just read, lines up with scripture; this is why it is widely accepted. God said that the 1000-year reign *(long earthly reign)* is literal and I believe that. This is a natural simple expression of the Biblical text, concerning the Book of Revelation. We believe the Church and Israel are separate. There is a future for Israel as we clearly see through this study of the Book of Revelation. The clear words of "one thousand years" are repeated six times in chapter 20, God's Plan keeps His Word true to Israel. **The "Church" when combined with "Old Testament Saints" & "Tribulation Saints" covers ALL of God's ELECT.** Those He chose before the foundation of the world; He will NOT lose any.

However, all of God's Elect will be Saved regardless of one's eschatological view, thank God! We *(Elect)* all believe in the same Gospel. **We *(Believers)* each had an**

encounter with God and were changed by God, that is NOT Poetry.

What some believers hold to be true eschatologically are combinations of the three main perceptions of the end times. **Before I completely read the whole Bible a few times from cover to cover, I was Amillennialistic in my baby Christian years.** Eschatology was ambiguous to me. There can be an argument made to a certain extent for each position. However, using Exegesis, my conclusions are Premillennial. This issue is not a Salvational issue. **Remember a pre-determined mind is sometimes a closed mind.** Therefore, it is vital to **study** the Book of Revelation, many times, which exhibits one's desire for Him.

The main difference concerning the three major "end time" views are arguably, **Amillennial**, **Postmillennial**, and **Premillennial** each conclude different interpretations. The differences revealed are much more than Revelation Chapter 20 verses 1-7, this references when Jesus is coming and what that truly means. There are many taking verses out of context and <u>falsely applying</u> them to support their particular stance, concerning their understanding of eschatology. This happens regarding all Biblical subject matter as well, beware. In other words, many will use the wrong Bible verse(s) whether knowingly or unknowingly to support their false narrative. Many apply irrelevant passages that look like they fit. However, these verses will speak of something concerning an entirely different subject matter. Therefore, many seem to look wise while they support their estranged and particular views. They use Bible verses that ONLY apply to The 2nd Coming of Jesus. However, most will confuse those verses and wist them to refer to The Rapture and vice ersa. This displays a confused person and ne who is trying to confuse you.

Moreover, all believers should examine ll scripture carefully. **Never blindly agree with anyone**. Many will twist God's Word to ave you side with them. **Examine all that I write here as well; all True Christians love**

correction. It has been through constant Biblical correction that God has allowed me to write several books. **You would be derelict in your duty as a Believer if you do not examine all you see, read, and hear concerning God's Word and His Standards.** All things considered; it is not wise to debate The Book of Revelation with false converts, and unbelievers. People who are not Born Again by God will only argue over everything, Biblical. It is so important to give out the Gospel, planting seeds of His Truths, always. The rest is up to God.

When you read my findings don't stop there, search and examine the scriptures for yourself. This is what the noble Bereans have done in *Acts 17.* **We must all treat scripture as the Bereans have.** What distinguishes God's Elect from everyone else is that they **believe in All of God's Truth and never want to exult their will over His.**

"Preach ELECTION and you will know who The Sheep and The Goats are."

A.W. Pink, *Bible Teacher*

Lastly, however, you differentiate the Book of Revelation, you must keep the Gospel central. As I write this book, I am thankful for His Word. My goal is to interpret The Book of Revelation fittingly, the best I possibly could concerning my understanding of what is revealed and what is not. These are the findings of my sincere and deep study of this book. I hope it has cleared up any confusion you may have or have had before its reading, in that, I pray.

"Every Christian is either a Missionary or an Imposter."

Charles Spurgeon, *Prince of Preachers*

"Are YOU doing it for God; or is it about YOU in Jesus's Name?"

Joseph Malara, *Theologian*

"To Preach a false gospel is to commit eternal murder."

James White, *Theologian*

Chapter 24

Eschatological Judgments

• **The 2nd Coming,** aka **Day of The Lord,** aka **Great and Dreadful Day of The Lord,** aka **The Day of Doom,** aka **The 2nd Advent.** This is when Jesus physically lands on Earth, after the seven years of Tribulation. He will bring His Wrath and Vengeance and Judge the unrighteous.

• **Sheol** aka **Hades**. This is a temporary holding place of punishment for the unredeemed *(lost)*, until **Final Judgment Day,** aka **The Great White Throne Judgment,** aka **Judgment Day.**

• **Final Judgment Day,** aka **Great White Throne Judgment,** aka **Judgment Day.** This is for all the unredeemed, unbelievers *(lost, false converts)*. This will happen after Christ's Millennium *(1000-year reign)* on Earth. **This day will bring ALL sinners who have ever lived, all together.** Those present for this day **will be thrown into HELL** aka **The Lake of Fire.** Hell, will be dreadful but not equally dreadful. There are levels of pain determined by one's works on Earth both good and bad. **It will always pay**

dividends to choose right over wrong during your life, even if not Saved by God.

• **Judgment Seat of Christ,** aka **Bema Seat of Christ.** This day is for all those Saved by God, His Elect. There will be Judgment for all Believers *(good and bad),* and rewards from Jesus will be given to those He deems worthy. **This is only for Believers *(God's Elect)* ...**

> **"The more like Christ you are the more the world will treat you like they treated Christ. Maybe you don't get much persecution because there's not much similarity."**
>
> John MacArthur, *Pastor-Teacher*

> **"There is NO WAY one can have a Born Again encounter with GOD and remain the same."**
>
> Joseph Malara, *Theologian*

Chapter 25

Comparison Between The Rapture and Jesus's 2nd Coming

• **Rapture:** The Elect *(The Church, His Bride)* will meet Jesus *(Bridegroom)* in the air, **not visible.**

• **2nd Coming:** Jesus returns to Earth with The Church and His angels; it is **very visible.**

• **Rapture:** Concerning the Rapture, the Mount of Olives will **not be touched**.

• **2nd Coming:** The Mount of Olives, will be **split in its middle**, Zechariah 14:4.

• **Rapture:** A very welcomed, **unknown time** Christians look forward to and the ultimate blessing for all Believers! **They *(we)* will not physically die!**

• **2nd Coming:** A written and **biblically calculated time** of great fear for the *Lost*, with death, and destruction. God's Wrath will be exhibited, **a time easy to gauge.**

- **Rapture:** The Earth remains **the same**.
- **2nd Coming:** The Earth **is transformed**.

- **Rapture:** The world is not yet judged, and the **world worsens daily** with sin and wickedness.
- **2nd Coming:** Sin is Judged Righteously and the **world will be renewed**.

- **Rapture:** Jesus comes, there is a shout, with the voice of the archangel and with the trump of God. However, this **will NOT be heard** by the unredeemed world. Furthermore, all those remaining on Earth will only see the after-effects of those who disappeared.
- **2nd Coming:** Heaven opens as Jesus comes vengefully to make war and to Judge. He will have countless angel armies and The Church with Him as well. He **will be unquestionably heard and seen**, *Revelation 1:7.* However, the

world will still not expect His coming. **He will come like a thief in the night.**

• **Rapture:** The reign of **The Antichrist is activated.** This will happen soon **after** the Rapture, **NOT before.** This is the start of "The Tribulation".

• **2nd Coming:** The reign of **Jesus is activated.** He will personally come down to Earth **7 years after** the start of The Tribulation.

• **Rapture:** The Saved *(Redeemed)* in their bodies go **up to Heaven**.

• **2nd Coming:** The saved **come back down** with resurrected new bodies, 7 years later.

• **Rapture:** This event has no precursor or warning signs, it is imminent. **He can come today**.

• **2nd Coming:** This event has many, many warning signs that are distinct **Biblical events that MUST happen first.**

• **Rapture:** This event is **ONLY for God's Elect**.

• **2nd Coming:** This event will **Save Israel**. It is also for the many who are **unredeemed**, on them God's Wrath will be served. There will also be a remnant of the newly redeemed *(Saved)* during The Tribulation, **Tribulation Saints.** Jesus will also set up The **New Jerusalem and His Millennial Reign.**

• **Rapture:** Again, this will transpire **before** The Tribulation.

• **2nd Coming:** Again, this will occur (7) seven years **after** the Rapture.

"It is ignorance of doctrine which is mainly responsible for thousands of professing Christians being captivated by the numerous fallacies of the day. It is but, doctrine properly received, doctrine studied with an exercised heart, will ever lead into a deeper knowledge of God and the unsearchable riches of Christ."

A.W. Pink, *Bible Teacher*

Poem Summary

The Poem you are about to read is the true account of my Christian conversion. I was home alone helplessly crying mightily in aching sorrow, with deep regret, regarding my sin. Hopelessly crying out concerning situations I could not fix, reverse, or change. This poem attempts to illustrate how God opened my eyes, softened my heart, and converted my mind and soul. He alone awakened me from being *Spiritually Dead* to being *Spiritually Alive* **In Him**. He gave me His Holy Spirit; it all happened in the blink of an eye. Certainly, from that moment on He gave me my newfound thirst for His Word and His Truths. I can only boast in Him; I had nothing to offer but sin and regret. The morning after that life-changing night, 20 years ago, went like this…I reached out to a "Christian" friend by phone the very moment I awoke, *(Pages 70-72)*, while still sitting at my bedside. The first question I asked him was, "How do you study the Bible?" He asked me "Do you have a Bible Concordance?" I replied to him, "Whatever that is, I will meet you in 45 minutes at the bookstore to get one." The rest is History…

Psalm 34:6 *This poor man cried, and the Lord heard him, and saved him out of all his troubles.*

God, I thought I Knew

On my knees desperately broken, crying out loud, out loud to a God I thought I knew, but didn't…

I cried hard "Take my life I have done nothing good with it" …nothing seemed to fit…

I cried and cried endless tears falling down my face, for my family gone, my shame, my guilt, my sin, knowing nothing would be the same, my life totally misplaced, but unbeknownst to me, there was much more I could not see…that would soon, take place…

I cried out "Take my life I have done nothing good with it," as my tears fell like heavy rain, I moaned and suffered with each grieving teardrop, greater and greater pain…

Alone in my anguish, sobbing uncontrollably, crying out loud to a God I thought I knew, but didn't…Unbeknownst to me…

I thought I was reaching out for God to hear me…but He was reaching down to me to be heard…

He said, "Read The Bible…Read My Word."

I clearly unmistakably heard…with my ears, my heart or a spiritual part? In the body or out…only God knows…

As chills rolled up and down my spine…was this all in my mind? No…I was in awe, and today I am still in it…a total surprise…as my tears immediately stopped flowing from my eyes…my heart skipped a beat, my eyes widened…Who, did I just meet?

I became quiet and still; it was clear to see…His Peace overcame me…

I was spiritually dead, until He said, what He said…

That night I went to sleep with a calm I never ever knew…woke with a Biblical thirst, so miraculously anew…

He Called me…now I do clearly perceive what I could never ever on my own…know, desire, or hunger to believe…

His plan for me that night, to un-blind me and give me His clear sight…up to then, I lived life recklessly through my foolish self-induced misery…crying out to a God I thought I knew…but didn't…Pretending to be a true believer but all the while, a self-deceiver…a make believer…

I am now all His, and His Good News I do tell…His Mercy Saved me from myself…and from an eternal Hell…Although that night, I begged Him to take, take my life…and, He did…

He took my old life and gave me New Life in Him…and took away my sin…I am now Born Again…through Grace by Him.

This is my testimony so true…the night I cried out…cried out to a God, I thought I knew…

In Closing

I deeply hope this simple book will make a sober difference in your life. I pray each reader is moved onto a more encouraging path Spiritually for Christ, where you delightfully set out to dig deeper into His Holy Word, daily. Remember to exegete His Word correctly and thoroughly as the Bereans did in the book of Acts. Throughout the past several months, my earnest focused study of The Book of Revelation has undoubtedly brought me much closer to God. My eyes and mind were opened wider to His Truths concerning His love for His Son Jesus, and little ole me, just one of His many Elect. Above all, I am astonished and in awe of how His last book has blessed my life moving forward. **This Book is the final Word of God until we meet.** I pray I have done the book of Revelation justice in my vibrant challenge to explain it. Undoubtedly, there is of course much conjecture concerning the unrevealed details that are yet to come. **Psalm 86:11** *Teach me thy way, O Lord; I will walk in thy truth: unite my heart to fear thy name.*

Lastly, one thing is certain, if you doubt your salvation, cry out to God, and don't stop. It is paramount that you read over and over The Gospel of John until God speaks back to your dead cold heart and brings His Life into it, cry out. He alone is Worthy…cry out for His Mercy. May The Grace of our LORD Jesus find you, grab YOU, and make you His, Amen. **Certainly, to all those who are Born Again by God, the Mission Field is plentiful and I encourage YOU to run your race to win...**

Notes